Unbounded Love

Unbounded Love

God and Man in Process

with study guide

by Norman Pittenger

A Crossroad Book · The Seabury Press · New York

The Seabury Press
815 Second Avenue
New York, N.Y. 10017

Printed in the United States of America

Library of Congress Cataloging in Publication Data

Pittenger, William Norman, 1905–
    Unbounded love.
(The First Stephen Fielding Bayne memorial lectures)
"A Crossroad book."
1. Theology, Doctrinal—Popular works—Addresses, essays, lec-
tures. 2. Process theology—Addresses, essays, lectures. I. Title. II.
Series: Stephen Fielding Bayne memorial lectures; 1st.
BT77.P56   230   76–2083   ISBN 0–8164–2119–6

In memory of
the Right Reverend Stephen Fielding Bayne
born 1908; died 1973

B.A., Amherst College; S.T.B. and
S.T.M., General Theological Seminary

Honorary doctorates from Amherst College, General Theological Seminary, Mills College, Whitman College, Columbia University, Australian Theological College, Hobart College, Puget Sound College, Saint Paul's College in Japan, Kenyon College, Harvard University, Huron College, Cuttington College in Liberia, Trinity College.

Deacon, 1932; Priest, 1933; Bishop, 1947

Fellow and Tutor, General Theological Seminary, 1932–34; Rector of Trinity Church, Saint Louis, Missouri, 1934–39; Rector of Saint John's Church, Northampton, Massachusetts, 1939–42; Chaplain of Columbia University, 1942–47; Chaplain, United States Naval Reserve, 1944–45; Bishop of Olympia, 1947–1960; Bishop-in-charge of European Convocation, 1959–64; Executive Office of the Anglican Communion, 1960–64; Director of Overseas Department of the Executive Council of the Episcopal Church, 1964–68; First Vice-President, Executive Council, 1964–1970; Professor of Christian Missions, General Theological Seminary, 1970–72; Dean of the General Theological Seminary, 1972–73.

Contents

Preface

The chapters in this book were originally the first of the Stephen Fielding Bayne Memorial Lectures, delivered in Saint Louis, Missouri, from March 17 to 20, 1975. They were prepared and given by invitation of a committee of St. Louisans who had known and esteemed Bishop Bayne while he was rector of Trinity Church in that city during the 1930s. Those who supported the lectureship included Trinity Church, Christ Church Cathedral, Emmanuel Church in Webster Groves, Eden Theological Seminary, and Webster College; and the lectures were delivered at the first three of these, while other talks were given at Eden Seminary.

When I was invited to prepare and deliver the lectures, I was asked that my topic should be "a theology for lay people." I have sought to fulfil this desire of the sponsoring committee, at the same time bearing in mind their admonition that the lectures should be sufficiently demanding of close attention and further thought, rather than simple in the sense of "simplistic."

As a member of and minister in the Anglican Communion, I have naturally spoken from my own stance, but the fact that the sponsorship included the United Church of Christ (through its seminary in Saint Louis) and the Roman Catholic Church (through Webster College) made it possible for me to speak ecumenically rather than denominationally. Furthermore, I have tried to be "radical" in the true sense of "getting at the root" of what Christians believe; certainly I did not wish to be either "reactionary," assuming everything has already been settled, nor "revolutionary," assuming that nothing can be learned from our Christian past and that we must begin all over again. How well I have succeeded in this attempt I cannot say, but at least my intention ought to be plain to the reader as I hope it was to the audiences, some very large and some rather smaller, who were kind enough to appear in the evenings and at the noonday sessions, during which the seven lectures were delivered.

I shall not try to name here the many persons who helped in the planning and who showed me much kindness and consideration but I must thank Richard and Sandra Tombaugh and their three children for hospitality and affection while I was their guest in Saint Louis. I must also express my gratitude for being asked to give the first of the lectures which are named in honor of an old friend who was also for a short time my colleague on the faculty of the General Seminary in New York many years ago.

NORMAN PITTENGER

King's College
Cambridge, England

Unbounded Love

I
Doing Theology Today

This book is intended to be an exposition of the basic affirmations of Christian faith. The material was prepared for delivery to gatherings of lay people and the lectures were given in honor of the late Bishop Stephen Bayne, an old and dear friend for many years. Stephen Bayne was an accomplished exponent of Christian theology for the laity of the Church; and with his example in mind, I sought to present to my audience a way of doing theology which would make contact with their minds, with their situation, and with the questions that seemed important to them. But I knew very well that one of the reasons for their invitation to me was their awareness that I myself had been for many years an exponent of a particular *way* of doing theology—the "Process" way.

That is why this introductory chapter will seek to present the main emphases in contemporary Process thought, a world view which more and more commends itself to thoughtful people especially in North America, and one which I believe makes sense of, and gives sense to, the ordinary experience of men and women who are not technical philosophers but simply people who must come to terms with the way things go in the world—and what is more, whose grasp of Christian faith becomes more real and more convinced when that faith is expressed in terms they can understand and accept.

Of course there are some who believe that it is possible to present the basic affirmations of Christian faith without the use of any more general world view. They think that the faith can stand on its own. Perhaps they are afraid of what they consider reliance on secular knowledge, assuming that somehow such reliance will damage the integrity of their religion. The truth is, however, that *everybody* without exception makes assumptions about himself, the world, and how things go in that world, assumptions which are "pre-conditions" for his religious convictions. Nobody is really without *some* world view—call it a "philosophy" if you wish—and that world view or philosophy will determine very largely how he sees religious faith, how he understands its implications, and how (when asked to do so) he would expound what he believes.

The early Christian thinkers whom we call the "Church Fathers" naturally assumed the view of things which was current in their own day: this was a variety of hellenistic or Platonic thought. In the Middle Ages, Saint Thomas Aquinas accepted, almost inevitably, the outlook associated with the name of Aristotle, whose writings had begun to be read in Europe. In the eighteenth century, Christian thinkers took for granted the prevalent ideas which scholars call "modern philosophy"—the influence of a Leibniz and a Descartes, for example, not to mention John Locke and others in Britain. In the nineteenth century, Christian thinking was usually in terms of the then widely accepted "idealism," often in its German expression through Hegel and in England through the influence exerted by the writings of Immanuel Kant. In our own century, the kind of theology sometimes styled "neoorthodoxy" is largely dependent upon the ideas of Kant and more recently on the "existentialism" which had its first clear exposition in the writing of Søren Kierkegaard, the great nineteenth-century Danish thinker who was rediscovered in the first four decades of this century. Karl

Barth and Emil Brunner are typical representatives of this "neoorthodoxy."

But what has all this to do with the ordinary man or woman who probably has read none of the great philosophers I have mentioned? The answer is quite simple. Even those who are not personally familiar with the work of such men are nevertheless influenced by them. Ideas somehow get around, often in a diluted form, and nobody can avoid them, try as hard as one may. In the nineteenth century, for example, "idealism" was in the air, taken for granted, assumed as evidently true. People talked about "ideals" and "values"; they felt them to be the most real of all real things. In our own day, the insight of "existentialism"—that each person is a responsible individual whose decisions establish him for what he is—is part of the mental equipment of many people, even if they would not for a moment think of calling themselves "existentialists."

It is my conviction that the general world view which *most* people today take for granted is more or less precisely what I mean when I speak of "Process thought." If that is the case, then this way of looking at things will provide a useful "handle," as we might put it, for our presentation of the great assertions of Christian faith. It will help to make that faith understandable because it will illuminate the fashion in which we can speak about ourselves, about the world, and about God. Therefore my task in this introductory chapter is to indicate the major emphases in Process thought, in the confidence that what is said will make contact with the experience of ordinary people and that a presentation of Christian faith in such terms will make sense to them.

Of course the faith itself is not a philosophy. But it most certainly presupposes a world view. If you are sure that the world is meaningless, or that its ultimate constituents are only bits of matter in motion, or that human existence is nothing more than a sort of irrelevant excrescence on the surface of the world, you will find it impossible to accept Christian faith. On the other hand, if there is good evidence for a world which has meaning, for the reality of talk about goodness and love or wickedness and hate, for human existence as possessing an abiding significance, then you will be prepared to listen to, if not to accept, the claims of religious and Christian faith. The faith comes to us through a long tradition, grounded in centuries of thought and experience; but the big question is: can we still believe what that tradition conveys? And if we can believe it, how can we work out its implications? In other words, how best can we do theology in our own day?

Let us now turn to a consideration of Process thought with a word or two about its origins. This conceptuality has a long ancestry but in recent times its greatest exponent was the Anglo-American philosopher Alfred North Whitehead, who taught at Cambridge University in England, then at London University, and during the last years of his life (he died in 1947) at Harvard University in the United States. Whitehead's book entitled *Process and Reality* gives the conceptuality its name. His best known exponent today is Charles Hartshorne, an American philosopher who was Whitehead's assistant at Harvard and then taught in Chicago, at Emory University in Georgia, and finally at the University of Texas, where he is still active and is continuing his writing. Further information about the background of Process thought may be found in two simply written books: *The Creative Advance* by Eugene H. Peters (Saint Louis: Bethany Press, 1966), and my own *Alfred North Whitehead* (Richmond: John Knox Press, 1969), both of them written for lay readers. A more advanced discussion can be found in my *Process Thought and Christian Faith* (New York: Macmillan, 1968), especially in the first chapter.

What do these two outstanding thinkers, Whitehead

and Hartshorne, and those who follow them in adopting the Process conceptuality, tell us about the world and ourselves? What they say may be summarized under nine points, all of them important and all of them making immediate contact with the experience of ordinary men and women.

1. The world in which we live is characterized by change. That world is not static, inert, unmoving; on the contrary, it is very much on the move. When you and I look at the world we see the changing of the seasons, the growing of trees and plants, the movement of dogs and cats. When we look into ourselves, we are immediately conscious that we too are changing creatures, from a past which in some sense we carry with us through decisions made in the present toward future goals or objectives at which we aim. We know that the human body renews itself every seven years, so that there is a continual process of alteration of cells; we know also that our ideas, beliefs, values, knowledge, and purposes are equally subject to modification as time goes on. There is process rather than an absolutely set and immutable grouping of things. The change we observe and experience is not always for the better; hence it would be wrong to speak of some inevitable progress. But then *process* and *progress* are words with different meanings. The former indicates the reality of movement; the latter indicates that movement is always for the better—and to think that such is the case is not only mistaken but absurd. Change may be for the worse, even if it may also be for the better.

2. If there is change there is also temporality. Time must be taken very seriously indeed. To change "takes time"; it is not an instantaneous matter. And it involves all three of the tenses: the *past* which has played its part in bringing us to the *present*, from which present we move toward the *future*, whether it be for better or for worse.

If we are in our senses, we know that we cannot deny the *past*, although we may use it in one way or another. We know that we are living in the *present*, where decisions must be made and where actions are undertaken—these may be large or small, apparently insignificant or obviously important, but they are facts of our experience which we cannot avoid. We know too that what we decide and do will have its effects or results in the *future* which is yet to come; and we know also that the future, when it comes, will lead on into further future states in which other decisions must be made and other actions undertaken. So it is that we see in the world around us and experience within ourselves the reality of past, present, and future; so it is that each of us must necessarily take temporal succession—the way things happen one after another, with all this entails—with the utmost seriousness. Nobody can escape from that succession into an imagined secure "timeless state."

3. The world (and we ourselves in that world) cannot be described in terms of hard, absolutely enduring, inert, changeless *things*. Robert Louis Stevenson's child's poem which spoke about the world being "so full of a number of things" is quite wrong; the world is made up of events or happenings. To put it picturesquely, the world is verbal, not substantival; it is constituted of activities and not of fixed entities. Modern physics has taught us that the final elements in creation are charges of energy, which arrange themselves in various kinds of patterning or forms; but it is the charges of energy which are the "really real" components. As Professor John Hick has suggested, "energy-events" constitute the world, not only of physics, but also of chemistry, zoology, botany, and biology. Recognition of this fact is now part of the mental equipment of all thoughtful people. Furthermore, such people know also that psychologically they are continuous chains of experience, adjusting and adapting themselves in various

ways but always aware of their existence as experiencing what they "encounter." Certainly each of us has his or her own identity as John or Mary or Louise; yet that identity is not given in some unchanging selfhood to which experiences are attached like clothes hung on a clothesline on Monday morning. Rather, personal identity is the name given to a remembered continuity between experiences in the past which are recalled in the present and aim toward future goals which (it is assumed) will in one way or another bring about fulfillment or satisfaction.

Sometimes these "puffs of experience" are focused in some pattern which appears fairly stable, just as the energy charges which make up the material world can give the appearance (say, in a table or a stone) of utter fixity. But the basic fact is that a table or a stone is a mass of activity, infinitesimally small to be sure but none the less very real. And the fact about ourselves is that we are made up of the experiences which we have, constituting us as this or that person who has a remembered and conscious continuity with earlier experiences and who looks forward to other experiences in the future.

4. In the world we know there is a very complicated interrelationship. Everything and everybody affects and influences everything and everybody else. What happens *here* will change what happens *there.* In the idiom usually adopted by Process thinkers, there is a grasping, feeling, or "prehension" of this by that, of that by this. So too with us in our human experience. John Donne wrote the famous lines "No man is an island entire of itself"; everyone, he said, belongs to the "continent" and hence everyone is influenced or affected by what happens to others—and by what happens in the world more generally, as well. The man or woman who tries to live as if he or she were not related to others is not only acting out a lie, but is also attempting the impossible. We all belong together, we all live together, we all have to do with each other. And what

is thus true of us, as any deep grasp of our own experience tells us, is true in its own way of everything else in the world. This is a *societal world;* it is not a simple heaping up of separate and entirely independent things or persons.

We might sum up the four points just made by saying that the world which we know, and we ourselves as existing in that world, can only rightly be envisaged as a changing world, where temporal succession is basic and where the elements which compose it are happenings or activities that mutually affect and influence one another, sometimes obviously, sometimes subtly, but always really and seriously.

5. The fifth point in our nine is the reality of freedom. Here it is not so much a matter of stressing that human beings have a certain degree of freedom of choice, although that is part of the story. Our concern is to assert that freedom, in the sense of a capacity for significant decisions which have consequences, runs straight through the creation. The word decision comes from the Latin verb *decidere,* whose meaning is "to cut off." To decide means, then, to do *this* rather than *that,* to move in one possible direction and therefore to "cut off" movement in another possible direction. Such freedom is radical in the whole creation, down to the lowest or least complicated events or actions.

In quantum physics we learn that when one of the energy-events of which the world is composed moves *this way,* it "cuts off" (here the word *decide* is important) its chance of moving in another way, which theoretically was open to it. There is nothing conscious about that decision, to be sure; none the less, it *is* a decision in the basic meaning of the word. As we move up in levels of created existence, there is an enhancement of such decision; at the animate level, perhaps, there is a glimmering of awareness however dim that may be. At the human level, as we all know, there is present a conscious sense of freedom, so that the agent knows that a choice is being made among possible courses of action. Of course all freedom has its limits. If I live, as I do, in Britain I cannot be free to choose as I might have done as a resident in Colorado. My situation, my inheritance, my education and cultural background, my family and its past, and much else in my experience will prescribe certain limitations upon my choosing. Nevertheless I am conscious that I *do* possess real, even if not unlimited, freedom to make significant decisions which are bound to have consequences for myself and for others, perhaps consequences for how the whole world will go in the future. The limits are set, we may well think, to prevent anarchy or chaos in what is plainly a cosmos or general orderly patterning; but the fact of freedom is deeply felt and its exercise is part of the experience of each one of us.

6. Each occasion or focus of energy-events has about it what many Process thinkers style a "dipolar" quality. That is to say, there are always two aspects or sides: the set of abstract possibilities, among which decisions must be made, on the one hand, and the actuality or the concrete decision and its consequences, on the other. In the former aspect, for example, I may have a whole range of opportunities which are open to me and of which I must take account. But in the latter aspect, I have chosen or I do choose this particular opportunity and I am what I am because of that decision. Abstractly I might even be said to include the whole of human existence as a potentiality with which I may deal; concretely I have done what I have done, I decide as I do decide, and I aim toward the goals or ends which I have felt to be most fulfilling or satisfying. By analogy we may say that this "dipolar" quality runs straight through the world, although obviously the analogy seems sometimes to be very remote indeed. The mere fact of existence is one thing; a particular *mode*

of existence is another—one is abstract and not definite, the other is definite and entirely concrete and specific.

7. Some events or actions, some occasions or happenings, are more "important" than others. The word *important* is itself important in this connection. Plainly whatever takes place has some importance, somehow and somewhere: "nothing walks with aimless feet," as the poet puts it. There is a value or meaning in any occurrence, although often enough that seems to be minimal and hardly worth noticing. But *some* occurrences strike us as being of quite special value and possessing quite particular significance. Most of us would think that our own human experience has such importance, at least for us, maybe also in a wider sense as well. When we come to interpret the world, we have every reason to assume that what we thus know in our experience is indicative of much else that is going on in the creation. If we are emergent from that natural order which is studied by the sciences of physics, chemistry, and biology, we rightly feel that it is better to interpret the prior and the lower levels by those which are later and higher. Man *is* an animal, as we know; but his consciousness and self-consciousness, his appreciation and his evaluation, his way of responding to challenges and opportunities, and much else which is distinctively human, can give an insight into what makes his animality different from that of "the beasts that perish"— and, as some of us believe, can also provide some clue to what was being worked out at earlier stages as the evolutionary process has continued through countless millennia.

As a matter of fact, there is really no other place to start than that provided by our concrete human experience. This is the one thing that we know intimately and with certainty; and it would be absurd to fail to take it most seriously and use it most carefully. The spectacle of human beings reducing their own experience to mere animality is funny; it is also pathetic. And the view of the world which results when this attempt is made is so unlike what we know at first hand that its absurdity is apparent —C. D. Broad's caustic words apply here, "There are some theories so silly that only a very clever person could have thought them up."

There is another aspect of this "importance," however. We all assume that certain moments in our own lives, certain events in the realm of human history, certain decisions made by men at one time or another, are important in that they have produced results which are much more than average. The time when I told someone I loved him or her, for example, will be important for us because it has established once and for all the direction our lives will take. Important events, in this sense, have an objective quality in that they are intensive and vivid in themselves and they also have a subjective quality in that they have had their enormous effects on what we feel will come afterward. To anticipate the discussion in a later chapter, Christians would say something like this about the event which we name when we speak of Jesus Christ: he is taken to be supremely important as a clue to how things go in the world, as an indication of what God is up to in the world, and as a representation of what human existence can be and is meant to be.

8. The eighth point in our list is the insistence that persuasion (or love) is stronger than sheer force or coercion. To many people this insistence may seem incredible. After all, they will ask, is it not apparent that force is the way in which things get done? And what about all the evil in the world and in human life, which any amount of persuasion seems unable to overcome? To these objections we may answer that, whatever may seem to be the case on a superficial and quick survey, our own experience knows that the most effective method of handling people and securing good results is not by sheer coercion

but by winning assent and securing cooperation. Whitehead once remarked that the history of human civiliza-
tion is the story of the slow, gradual, but certain victory
of persuasion over force. This does not entail the notion
that everything is getting better, the idea that "every day
in every way things are getting better and better," as M.
Couè, the French quack psychologist, put it years ago. Of
course this is not the case. For every advance in civiliza-
tion, there is always a possible, perhaps even a probable,
chance of slipping back; in any event, "the higher you
may rise, the further you may fall."

What is at stake here is something which the history of
the world's religions plainly demonstrates. Slowly but
surely, over the passing centuries, these religions have
come to put persuasion or love before coercion or force.
The ninety-nine "Names of God" which Muslims recite
end with God as "compassionate"; and the development
of Islam has been away from stress on sheer power to
stress on that compassion. The terrible aspects of the divine in Hinduism's earlier days give place to the care of
God for his creatures as expressed in the *Bhagavad-Gita*.
Gautama Buddha moved from recognition of the sheer
mystery of existence to the teaching that fellow-feeling
and sympathy is the key to the good life. In China the
almost fatalistic "Heaven" of an earlier period was re-
defined by Confucius and others for whom goodness expressed in human relationships was recognized as being
the "purpose of Heaven" whose ultimate character was
benevolent and not cruel, caring rather than fatalistically
indifferent. As we shall see, Judaism also moved from the
terrifying Yahweh of pre-Mosaic days to the stress by the
great prophets on *hesed* or lovingkindness as the true
nature of the God whom they worshiped.

That which is revealed in this brief summary is plain
enough: somehow the heart of man and his reading of the
significance of his experience, even in the midst of suffer-

ing and evil, cannot accept a view of life which gives coercive action priority over persuasive or loving concern. Furthermore, in our common experience we see the working out of this belief in concrete practice: only the *winning* of the other will be effectual in overcoming the other's tendency toward selfishness. You cannot *make* somebody respond to you in love; you *can* lure him or her to respond in that way, by yourself being a caring person whose whole activity toward the other is characterized by a love that "will not let him go." Here, if anywhere, the importance of deeply human experience has much to tell us about what is "important" in the world, in the long run and through patient and often painful outgoing of love.

9. Our last point is the affirmation that if we are going to talk about God at all, we must do it in terms which are not the denial of the preceding principles but rather their "chief exemplification" (to use a phrase of Whitehead's). The word *God* is not self-explanatory; it can mean a great variety of things, some of them terrible, some immoral, some absurd, and some of them enriching, ennobling, and magnificently evocative. For us, any model or picture or concept of God which is to make sense must be one that includes his self-identification with a processive world, his serious use of time and his existence as sharing in temporal succession (even if not exactly as we finite creatures know it), his being as active and alive, his relationship with all that is not himself, his freedom for decision amongst relevant possibilities, his "dipolar" nature as including both abstract existence and actual concrete selfhood, his expressing or revealing himself in particular events which thus acquire "importance," and (above all and first of all) his character as sheer Love-in-action.

The followers of Process thought who have concerned themselves with religious matters have worked hard during the past few decades to develop a picture or model or

conception of God that will fulfil these requirements. In
doing this, they have discovered that they were in fact
developing a theology which had remarkable affinities
with the biblical portrayal of God. Of course this would
not be the case if the biblical material had been interpreted in a literalistic fashion, taking no account of the way
the portrayal developed over the centuries of Jewish and
then Christian experience. But because such thinkers
have been prepared to accept gladly, if not uncritically,
the approach to Scripture which two centuries of careful
scholarship have provided for us, they have been remark-
ably successful in showing that this biblical way of speaking of deity fits admirably with the Process approach—or,
from the stance of Christian thinkers, that the Process
conceptuality fits into and gives its added significance to
the way the Bible speaks of God, from the primitive
awareness of the earliest nomadic tribes through the con-
tributions of Moses and the prophets to the culmination
of that long history in the person, the activity, the teaching, and the meaning of Jesus of Nazareth.

How then should a Christian *use* this Process approach?

First of all, it should be clear that he cannot carve the
inherited faith of the Christian centuries so that it will
nicely adjust itself to this, or any other, secularly derived
way of seeing things. To do that would be to damage
irretrievably the integrity of the Christian witness. But if
there is, as I have argued, a genuine "fit" between the
two, he will be prepared to use it, so far as it goes. If he
does this, he will discover that much in the inherited faith
is illuminated and that new insight is given into many
hitherto neglected elements of that which we have received.

Furthermore, a Christian will know that there can
never be a *final* theology, true now and for all time.
Unhappily, some theological conservatives talk as if "the
faith once delivered to the saints" is identical with the

formulations of that faith made by great thinkers in the past—whether it be Thomas Aquinas or John Calvin or Martin Luther, or even earlier thinkers like Augustine. Theologies are man-made; they are our best attempts to make an articulate statement of what the commitment to God in Christ tells us about God and man and the world. We ought to expect and welcome new theological formulations, provided always that they are faithful to that basic commitment without which no one can rightly claim to be called Christian.

The Process perspective will help us to see that no sound Christian theology can fail to take as its basic criterion of all that is said the clear insistence that God is primarily Love-in-act. Everything else that is said must qualify that affirmation; whatever is inconsistent with it must be rejected. Process thought will help us to see that God is active in the world and self-identified with it. Hence it will reject the idea that God is somehow statically timeless; rather, it will accept that he is involved in temporal succession and that in his own divine life time matters. It will enable theology to recognize and gladly accept the value of human existence, in its freedom and responsibility, and will not try to push off onto God all responsibility for what happens in the world. Again, it will make it possible for the theologian to make sense of the biblical view that not only is God disclosed in what happens in the world but also is affected by what happens there, both rejoicing in creaturely joy and sharing in creaturely anguish.

Because of the stress on "importance," Process thought will assist us in understanding how Jesus can be the decisive "act of God in human history." This can now be done without denying the more pervasive or general activity of God in the affairs of the world, while at the same time the *focal* disclosure in Jesus Christ can be given its proper place and significance. The Process way of seeing human nature will open the way to a grasp of the implicit Christian conviction that man is being created, through his own "en-graced" decisions and actions, in such a way that he may move toward "the image of God in manhood," which is to say toward both reflecting and representing the cosmic Love that is God himself. And finally, such Process thought can help to make it clear that human destiny itself is in God, where the human contribution will be in making available to God yet another personalized agency for further growth in creaturely goodness and love and for the overcoming of evil and wrong.

Thus there will be no contradiction between the fullest recognition of human existence and the acceptance of the reality of God and God's working in the world.

If the world view associated with the Process conceptuality is adopted and the consequences which follow from this, so far as Christian concerns are in the picture, are also accepted, what sort of theology will be necessary? The chapters which follow are an attempt to answer these questions.

From one point of view, the general structure of Christian theology will remain as we have inherited it. This is inevitable, since there are abiding emphases and convictions which make that theology an identifiable reality: God as supremely worshipful and utterly caring; Jesus Christ as the expression of God in human history; the gift of the empowering Spirit who continually renews and enables human life; the community of faith and discipleship; the sacramental means of relationship with God; and a destiny in which human existence finds its ultimate fulfillment in God himself. Were these emphases and convictions absent, we should not have Christian faith at all; hence, we should not have a theology which would merit the name Christian either.

But from another point of view, everything is changed, once we have adopted the Process world view and have

accepted the consequences which follow from it. Why is
this the case? The answer is that a new perspective, a new
slant on things, always produces different results. The old
is now seen in a new light. Ancient and inherited affirmations are set in a new context—and, as we all know, it is
certainly true that new contexts bring about difference in
content. An ancient Christian writer, Vincent of Lerins,
once said that he was seeking "not to say new things, but
to say the old things in a new way." What he failed to
realize was that if one does say things, whatever they may
be, in a "new way," the inevitable result is that they will
become "new things" insofar as they are seen and interpreted in a new fashion. If one turns a precious stone so
that the light catches it in a different fashion, it will reveal
facets of the stone that had not previously been seen.
There will be the old beauty, to be sure, but it will be
differently perceived and differently enjoyed.

So it is, to my mind, with the "re-conception" of Christian theology through the use of Process ways of looking
at the world. The patterning of our theology will not be
the same as that familiar in the past, yet the faith which
the theology seeks to articulate and express will be the
same. We may anticipate what will follow in later chapters by citing two examples. One has to do with the involvement or self-engagement of God in the created
world. Instead of a wholly transcendent and remote deity,
we shall have to do with God as active in and present
through the whole of creation; divine transcendence will
be interpreted, not in terms of "remoteness," but in terms
of the utter inexhaustibility of God's resources of loving
care and concern. The other example is the placing of
love at the very center of the theological picture. Instead
of defining God in terms of sheer being or primarily as
first cause, we shall think of God as "pure unbounded
Love" (in Charles Wesley's phrase which we shall have
occasion to mention time and again) and perceive that

whatever else we may need to say must be a corollary of
the divine Love or at least entirely congruous with that
Love. Thus we shall not be content to say, as many have
done, that love is one of the "moral attributes of God" but
only one among many other attributes. On the contrary,
we shall be obliged to affirm with the First Letter of John
that "God *is* Love"; or to put it otherwise, that God's
is-ness, the divine being itself, is nothing other than this
Love—and we shall find it necessary to capitalize the
word *Love* and to personalize it too. For us to say "God"
will also be to say "cosmic Lover," and to speak about God
will be to speak about the One whose love is the very
essence of his selfhood, a love that is universal in its scope
and particular in its application to each and every aspect
and area of the world and of human existence in the
world.

Now we may proceed to spell out a theology for lay
people in which the Process conceptuality provides what
earlier in this chapter we called the "handle" for a Christian understanding in our own time. In doing this, we shall
follow the usual scheme or ordering of theology: God,
man, Christ's person and accomplishment, Christian community, the sacramental life, and the question of human
destiny.

II
God

Several years ago in Britain, where I now live, a controversy arose in one of the political parties about the interpretation of a section of the party's organizational statement. A leader said that there was no reason for worrying about the interpretation; the matter, he said, was "merely theological." In the context it was clear that what the politician meant was that it was only a question of theory or speculation. But his use of the word *theological* may be taken as an indication of a very widespread notion: namely, that things which really do not matter much, which are essentially only theory or speculation without any serious impact on important questions and the way decisions are to be made about them, constitute the topic upon which theologians may ponder but which have no genuine significance for ordinary people.

We must admit that often enough this has appeared to be the case. And we must go on to admit that frequently theologians have indeed concerned themselves with issues that have little if any relevance to daily living. But when this happens, theologians are being untrue to their essential task; and when we accept such a dismissal of the meaning of theology we are victims of a very grave misunderstanding. For theology is nothing more, nothing less, than a concern with God and with God's ways in the world; and once anybody admits that God *is* and that his ways in the world *are* of crucial importance, then theology becomes highly significant—and what is more, everybody is seen to have a theology of some sort, be it good or bad.

Of course when we say, as I have just done, that "God is" and that "his ways in the world are of crucial importance," we have to inquire exactly what we mean by the word *God* and exactly what we are discussing when we speak of his *ways*. But to engage in such an inquiry is to "do theology." Asking about what or who God is, concerning ourselves with his activity and its meaning, is the first step in theology. And it can be said that every human being who stops for a moment to think about self, about the world, and about what matters most in his or her human existence, is thereby occupied with theological questions, even if in the end his or her conclusion is that there is no God at all and that any discussion of divine activity and purpose is simply beyond human capacity or, at the worst, nonsensical and absurd.

Unhappily a great many lay people seem to assume that "theology is not for them," as they might put it. The specialists, professional theologians in theological schools or other places, are the ones who should bother about these issues. Laypersons, they think, need not concern themselves about such issues; *their* business is to get on with the job of living out whatever faith they may happen to profess. But to think or talk in that fashion is to set up an intolerable barrier between faithful living and careful thinking—in other words, to run the risk of having a thoughtless religion, on the one hand, or a dead and irrelevant engaging in ideas, on the other. Today, more than ever before, we are conscious of the need for full cooperation between experts and ordinary people; and those of us who are Christians are, or ought to be, keenly aware of the way in which the *whole* Body of Christ, which is the Church, should work together to bring about a reasoned and reasonable understanding of the faith and at the same time a devoted discipleship to the Lord about whom that faith speaks and to whom all Christians, without exception, are committed.

At the same time, if we *are* to grasp the abiding Christian faith and make sense of the convictions which we have received from the past or which we have made our own in this day, we need to be open to new ways of seeing the world and man, new ways of stating the reality of the God with whom we have to do, and also new ways of affirming the enduring truths to which Christianity is entirely and utterly dedicated. Many of the older ways have had their day and have ceased to be helpful to us; many of them, if we are honest with ourselves, say nothing much to us today, perhaps are incredible, and may even be nothing but misrepresentations of the real, central, and abiding insights of Christian faith.

To say this is to admit that engaging in theology is a risky business; we can no longer remain "at ease in Sion" but must dare to venture out in ways different from those which our ancestors in Christian faith found helpful, meaningful, and compelling. Thus what we are undertaking here is not the simple re-affirmation of old ideas but a genuine and serious re-conception or re-thinking. And I invite you to share with me both the risks and the glory of such an enterprise: the risks, because (as I have said) we may find ourselves compelled to give up things that have seemed precious; the glory, because nothing could be more thrilling and enlivening than to discover for ourselves, and make our very own, the deepest truth of what the philosopher Alfred North Whitehead once called "the Galilean vision" and what that vision tells us about "God's nature and his agency [or activity] in the world."

We begin, then, with *God*. This may seem very strange to some for whom Christianity is a "way of life" which

naturally includes mention of God and obedience to
God's supposed will but which essentially is a human enterprise, an ethical attitude, or a mode of social relationships which they find enriching and enabling. I wish to
insist, however, that Christianity is basically a life which
is lived in relationship to the way in which things *really
go* in the world—and that means in relationship to what
God is "up to" and is accomplishing in that world. This
cannot be ignored no matter how difficult it may be to see
this clearly and no matter how many difficulties—like the
facts of evil, suffering, and wrong, facts so obvious to us all
—we may have to face in speaking about God and his
ways with humankind. Christianity is essentially a theocentric, or God-centered, way of life. That ought not to
suggest that it is not seriously concerned with us human
beings and our existence here and now; on the contrary,
it is deeply concerned. But its concern is with what gives
that existence its true value and makes human living rich
and important.

Now we must ask the question: if God *is,* how are we
to think about God? Or put in another fashion, what picture of God are we to entertain? Or, for a third way of
stating it, what is our model for God? These are different
phrasings of the same basic issue, which is the conception
of God that is appropriate for those who hold to Christian
faith. It is precisely at this point that we come to see the
organic nature of Christianity. By this I mean, the manner
in which the various affirmations or convictions held by
Christians through the ages are interrelated, so that each
one of them is affected by, and in its turn affects, all the
others. Nowhere is this so apparent as in the business of
conceiving what and who God is. For at the heart of Christianity there is the strong and enduring commitment of
the believer to Jesus Christ; and this is not to Jesus simply
as a Jew of the first century who taught religious and
moral truths. Obviously Jesus was, historically speaking, a

Jew who lived in Palestine during the first century of our
era. But for Christian belief he is something else, too; and
that something else is of crucial importance. He is the
disclosure or revelation, the expression or manifestation,
of God himself—in traditional language he is the specific
incarnation of God in human history.

Hence, when we want to speak of the Christian conception or picture or model of God, Jesus Christ must come
to occupy a central place. What was disclosed, revealed,
expressed, manifested in and through *him* is the clue to
the very reality of God; in and through him, says the
Christian, we are given a key to our understanding of who
God is, what God is up to, what is the nature or character
of the most real, profound, and vital thrust or drive in the
whole cosmos. But since nobody can say everything in one
moment, we cannot give proper attention to that great
Christian affirmation until and unless we have said something first about the God who *is* thus declared in Jesus and
also about the human creatures, you and me, to whom
that God is thereby revealed and in whose idiom and
existence the revelation took place. For the present, then,
we shall make but two statements about "God *in Christ,*"
postponing until a later chapter a more detailed and adequate discussion of the perennial Christian belief in Christ
as both the incarnation of God in humankind and the
means by which God and humans are brought together in
a saving or reconciling fashion.

The two statements which must here be made are: first,
that if God is indeed "in Christ," as Paul puts it, then God
is an active and living God who does not exist in isolation
or separation from the world and from human history;
and second, that if God is disclosed in Christ, he is disclosed as one whose "nature and name is Love." The
living God is the loving God; the Love which is the most
real and profound drive or thrust in the cosmos is nothing
other than the *Lover,* the One who, as personal and self-

communicative, actively cares for, is ceaselessly related to, and self-identified with, the world which is *his* world. Nowhere is this double truth so plainly spoken as in the First Epistle of John, where the author tells us that "God is love" and that we know this to be true, not because we have thought it up but because God has himself *acted lovingly:* "In this was manifested the love of God toward us, because that God sent his only begotten Son into the world, that we might live through him" (4:8–9).

I suggest to you, therefore, that at the very heart of the Christian faith is the bold assertion that life and love are coincident in the One whom men are to worship, obey, and seek to serve. The universe is the place where such living Love is at work, despite all that would seem to tell against any such belief. Anything else that we may wish to say about God must be congruous with *that* affirmation; it must be a consequence of it or an implication which follows from it.

Oddly enough, Christians have often found it difficult to take this attitude. Historically speaking, they have been altogether too ready to begin with some other picture of God and then to introduce, as a qualification, the notion that his character is a loving one. In a way this was both natural and inevitable. When the first Christians began to work out for themselves a coherent statement of the faith by which they lived, they were influenced by the then prevalent notions in the Graeco-Roman world in which they lived. Of course they had the Jewish conception of God to start with; that ought to have taught them that God must be pictured as dynamic, living, active, and concerned with creation. And of course their own deep faith in God disclosed in Jesus made it plain to them that somehow or other God loved his world and his human children. They did not forget either of these, but they tended to "model" God, as we might phrase it, in terms of the "unmoved mover" of Greek thought. What is more, they had only one notion of sovereignty or rule, a notion that inevitably they picked up from their knowledge of the dictator-kings of the world of the time. So when they wished to state that the God in whom they believed was both creator of the world and the supreme power in the world, they stated their belief in language which reflected those prevalent notions: unmoved mover and first cause, on the one hand, and omnipotent controller of everything that happens in the world, on the other.

The tragedy is that as Christian thinkers went on with their work they tended to emphasize more and more the ideas which were not derived from Jewish religion nor clearly implied in the loving activity they knew to have been operating in the total person and work of Jesus. That is to say, the picture of God which became increasingly dominant was not based firmly and unmistakeably on the living and loving God of their working religion, but on the more speculative views of philosophers who talked about "first cause" or "absolute being" and on the uncriticized portrayal of dictatorial control, sheerly omnipotent power, or tyrannical rule which they saw in the governments and the petty states of the then-known world roundabout the Mediterranean basin. At the same time, they could not help believing firmly that, in some inexplicable manner, that same God was truly the loving Father about whom Jesus had spoken.

Perhaps we could put it simply by observing that much of Christian theology has had a schizophrenic character. On one hand, the actual religion by which men lived and in whose terms they prayed and adored; and on the other hand, the speculative ideas which they accepted without question from Graeco-Roman philosophy: these two were held in an uneasy combination. One of the remarkable facts of recent years has been the recovery of the former of these two—God as the living and loving cosmic drive —as the essential point in a truly Christian world view. In addition, contemporary Christian thinkers have at last come to see that when that centering of attention on "living and loving" is seriously pursued, a total interpretation of the world and humanity and God not only may be, but can be, constructed which satisfies our intellectual demand for clarity, coherence, and consistency, and at the same time makes sense of, and gives sense to, the deliverances of practical faith as we engage in worship, prayer, and discipleship to Jesus Christ.

I wish now to approach this matter from a consideration of the sort of world which nowadays we know to be ours. There are three or four patent truths about that world, previously mentioned in chapter one, which are entirely inescapable for any observant and thoughtful person. These truths include the recognition of the dynamic quality of everything, literally everything. Ours is a world which is "in process'; and every bit of it, including you and me, is to be seen as just that: "a process" which is simply the reality of change, movement, development (for good or for ill). Evolution biologically speaking, change in physical matter, directive activity in psychological terms, are all obvious facts with which we must reckon.

In the second place, the ultimate constituent elements in this world are not *things,* easily located and situated at given times and places. Rather, they are "events" or "happenings," constellations or focusings of energy. This book, for example, is not a solid inert thing; it is a complex aggregation of charges of energy which only *appears* to be a solid and inert thing. Above all, you and I are not static finished articles; we are routings or chains of experienced occurrences or occasions, held together as a unity by memory and anticipation or the entertaining of goals or ends toward which we aim.

Thirdly, everything in the world is related to everything else; everything affects or influences everything else; everything is dependent upon everything else. Ours is a "societal world," so that whatever happens *here* has its affect upon its context *there*. When you toss a pebble into a pond, ripples go out to the remotest part of the pond. So it is, physicists tell us, that a simple act like dropping a pencil on the floor has repercussions throughout the whole universe. It may not look that way, to be sure; but that is the way it is. What is true of inanimate things is even more true in the living organism; every part of our body is related intimately with and has influence upon every other part. And in our human contacts this is much more obviously the case. If I may quote again the celebrated and extremely pertinent words of John Donne: "No man is an island, entire of itself"; on the contrary, he or she belongs to and can only be understood in relationship with other humans in the great community of humanity.

Finally, there is a purposive quality running straight through the whole creation. Acorns grow into oak trees; this we know very well, but perhaps we do not quite so frequently see that even in the world of electrons and atoms and molecules there is a drive, not consciously entertained of course, to fulfil the possibilities inherent in each bit of matter. At the human level, there is an aim or goal toward the achievement of which we exist, since on the basis of the past which we carry about with us and in the light of the decisions we make in the present, we move toward or we move away from the making real of whatever human potentialities are ours.

Dynamism, energetic activity, interrelationship or sociality, and the trend towards goals: these are characteristics of every part of the world we know. Scientists of all schools, philosophers of many different allegiances, thoughtful men and women considering their own life pattern, all agree about this; and maybe this agreement about the dynamic, energetic, societal, and goal-directed nature of the world is one of the most remarkable features of the world view common to people of every type and background in the civilized world of our day.

We shall have occasion to apply these characteristics to the assertions of Christian faith as they refer to humanity and Christ, to the Holy Spirit, to the Church and the sacraments, and to human destiny and cosmic fulfillment. At the moment, however, I wish to urge that they must be applied, first of all, to our conception of God. The basic drive or thrust in and behind everything, taken in Christian faith to be the living and loving God, is also to be understood as supremely personal, dynamic, and active (that, indeed, is what we mean when we speak of "the living God"). God is no static or inert "being" but is a continuing and enduring process or movement (for that is what we mean when we speak of God's purpose as being really God himself, not something "added to him," so to speak). God is societal or constantly related to the world and its ongoing (that is what we mean when we say that God is Love, because love *is* nothing other than relationship at its most intense and caring). And God is aiming at goals or ends (which is what we are talking about when we speak of God's "bringing in his kingly rule" or "establishing his kingdom" in the world).

What is so astonishing that it would seem to be, as I believe it is, intended and inescapable is the way in which the picture of God as living Love—or to put this in more personal terms, the living Lover—and the picture of God as dynamic, energetic, relational, and goal-directed fit together to make *one* picture. It is rather as if two sets of belief, two portrayals derived from different sources, came together to give us a single unitary vision. Nor should this be surprising to us, once we have accepted the belief that God is the God of the *whole* world, not just of one bit or portion of the world.

The God with whom we have to do is *this* God: not some remote speculative first cause; not some supposedly unmoved origin of all things; not a tyrannical dictator who controls almost automatically what takes place. On the contrary, *this* God is the dynamic, energetic or active, living, related, purposive, loving One—in fact, the God of whom the Bible speaks. In the Bible, to be sure, this speaking is in highly poetical and imaginative idiom, sometimes with the use of ideas which we can no longer accept in anything like their immediate and obvious significance. The Bible is a great anthology whose parts include history, drama, moral teaching, religious aspiration, and the like. It tells us how one particular group of people, over a long period of time, came to deepen their first discernment of the character and action of God in the world. It is not a theological textbook but a great storybook; yet the story is not based upon fiction or theory, but upon happenings which forced men and women to respond and then to think out what those happenings, when responded to, really signified.

In conclusion I want to put special stress on the Christian certitude that God is Love. Often this is forgotten or minimized, as I have said; but all the time it is the absolutely basic conviction which lives at the heart of the entire Christian tradition when those who share in that tradition are genuinely appropriating and actualizing the "Galilean vision" of which Whitehead spoke. The divine Love is not sentimentality, easy toleration, cheap and undemanding acceptance of anything and everything. It is very different indeed; the divine Love is sheer self-giving, sacrificial activity, suffering concern, enduring joy, readiness to accept and receive from others—some glimpses of which we have seen in our own limited, finite, and defective experience of human relationships that are true and sound and good, open and wholesome, enriching, enabling, and up-building.

In those moments when we are truly at one with another, in sheer self-giving and gracious receiving, in mu-

tual effort, in the anguish and the ecstacy of genuine union of lives, we come as close as ever we can come to the
heart of Godhead. That is why it is entirely natural and
proper to think of human persons as "lovers in the making," intended to move in their loving towards the divine
Love whose very image and action in the world is seen in
the human love which was Jesus Christ. Because in him
that human love was thus so supremely visible, it makes
sense to speak of him as also the one in whom the divine
Love was embodied, expressed, "en-manned," supremely
and as adequately as we can conceive possible.

III
Man

Christian faith is essentially theocentric. That is, Christians place their faith, their confidence and their trust, in what I called the deepest, most real, cosmic thrust or drive—in God. They see this drive or thrust as living, dynamic, energetic, continually in relationship with the rest of things, working toward achieving a goal or purpose. Above all, they see this drive or thrust as characterized by love, so much so that it is a basic Christian conviction that God *is* Love or Lover—*Lover* because the Love which is central in the whole fabric of things is personalized, to be addressed because known as a personal reality.

At the same time, Christian faith is deeply concerned with man, man's nature, man's purpose, man's destiny. It sees human beings as children of God, who cares for them as a "loving heavenly Father" for those who are his sons and daughters. I have just said "beings," but in the following I shall urge that none of us is *a being,* if by that we signify a finished article; on the contrary, each of us is *a becoming.* We are on the way toward a fulfillment of our human potentialities or we are moving away from such fulfillment and toward a very different goal, the denial or negation of this fulfillment. In its concern with human existence, Christian faith is prepared to make the highest claim for humanity—namely, that we are being created, both by our own decisions and by gracious influence and

persuasion from God, toward reflecting in our own existence something of the Love which is God. Since God is
the cosmic Lover, men and women who are his sons and
daughters are intended to move toward the image of God
in humanity: to express through their human loving, in
company with their fellows, the divine Loving which is
God's nature and character.

Thus the Christian view of human nature is not, as so
many seem to have thought it to be, a denial of its dignity
and value. Neither is that view utterly pessimistic, seeing
humans as so sunk in sin and so alienated from their true
fulfillment that there can be no hope for them. Certainly,
as we shall have occasion to note, human life is defective,
marked by wilful self-assertion and disregard of others
and by false self-centeredness with the pride and arro-
gance which are its consequence. So men are "sinners,"
as traditional religious language puts it. But at the same
time they are capable, however feebly, of making *some*
response to the divine Lover. Through the gracious influence of that Lover, which traditional religious language
knows by the word "grace," they may be set on the right
path and enabled to move forward toward the realization
of their destiny as human lovers. About all this we shall
have more to say.

At the moment, however, it will be helpful to set down
in a series of brief statements the chief ingredients of the
Christian view of human nature. These statements are
drawn from the general biblical picture, brought to its
culmination in the humanity of Jesus Christ who is "the
proper Man," as Martin Luther put it—humanity in its
real nature, as God would have humans to be. They are
also drawn from what we have learned through secular
observation, investigation, and thought over many centuries, and not least in recent years thanks to the development of psychological insight, sociological understanding,
biological observation and experiment, and other chan-

nels through which our knowledge has been enormously expanded and our grasp of what it means to be human has been given a new slant and a new interpretation. Of course what is intended when we speak of the Christian view of human nature is not simply a repetition of what our ancestors have said, although that is very important and must never be forgotten. The Christian view, as held today by Christian thinkers of all sorts, from many denominations, and with diverse backgrounds and training, includes also an awareness and use of quite contemporary information, not accessible to our ancestors but readily available for us today. In respect to humankind, just as much as in respect to the character of God, we can be like those householders of whom Jesus spoke, who bring out of their treasure things both old and new. To combine old and new is to be alive; and Christian thought today is very much alive.

The first point about human nature, to which I have already referred, is its dynamic quality. A human, I said, is not so much a "being" as a "becoming." When we look deeply into ourselves and when we observe other people, we cannot rest content with the notion that we are here as entirely completed creatures, of whom a sketch might be made along the lines of those diagrams people sometimes make of a machine; neither are we to be described as if a cross-section of our present condition were all there is to be said. No. We are, we feel ourselves to be, and we notice that other people are, "on the move." Physiologists tell us that in seven years the cells of our bodies are completely renewed, so that in one sense at least we are quite new creatures at the completion of that period of time. But the same is true, in another sense, of *all* of us.

We inherit from our past a great deal which we remember consciously; we inherit also a great deal that is deep in our subconscious, as contemporary depth psychology has taught us to recognize. There is still another, even deeper, kind of memory; that is the way in which our whole organism, physiological as well as psychological, carries the past which has been ours—what has happened to us and in us and with us is never entirely lost but is always active (to a greater or less degree) in our present. We live in the present moment, surrounded by a world of people and what we style (inaccurately, as I have urged) "things" in that world. These make their impact upon us as we make our impact upon them. Finally, we also live toward a future, in which we are going to become something—what that is we may not know in detail but it is something which in a general sort of way we do grasp: the making real of the possibilities which are integral to us as human processes. Our human existence is a dynamic routing from the past, through the present, toward the future; and we never understand ourselves, nor can we understand other people, unless we take this dynamic, processive, directional quality very seriously.

At the same time we have an identity. Each of us is him or herself and nobody else. What is it that constitutes this identity which makes me myself and you yourself? I suggest that it is our *conscious awareness* of that past, that present, and that future, about which we have just been speaking. Somewhere along the line of general evolutionary advance, some complex bits of matter which had become animate acquired the new quality of awareness of their routing or movement. They knew, unquestionably and plainly, that each of them was *this* particular continued routing of happenings, experiences, or occurrences. We shall see later how such awareness of selfhood is dependent upon awareness of others; at the moment I wish only to stress both the process of human becoming *and* the consciousness which men and women possess of a self that is indelibly theirs, distinct from the selves of others.

In the second place, each human being (and I must use

this inaccurate term because it happens to be both convenient and conventional) is not independent of but dependent upon the world in which he or she is set. We are necessarily dependent upon that world. We need food and drink, shelter, all sorts of provisions and all sorts of providing, so that we can grow and develop. Indeed the whole world is like that, in being a dependent world which neither explains its own origin nor explains its own present existence. Ultimately we are dependent upon the deep and enduring thrust which we call God; "it is he that hath made us and not we ourselves," as the Psalmist wrote. Anybody who sets out to be entirely independent is acting a lie; he is guilty of appalling presumption because he has fallen into the state which the English agnostic Bertrand Russell once called "cosmic impiety." Russell was certainly an agnostic, if not an atheist (at least so far as that meant denying the ideas of God which he assumed religious people hold); at the same time he was a man of great perception and could not fall victim to the fallacy of utter human independence of anything and everything else. Neither should we.

Thirdly, each human being is a mysterious and complex association of bodily stuff and mental awareness. One way of putting this would be to say, with Evelyn Underhill, "In this narrow bed [of human personhood] spirit and sense are wed." The marriage is not always a happy one, since sometimes Brother Ass, as Saint Francis of Assisi called our body, wants to run the show and sometimes our mind or spirit wishes to deny that body altogether. Neither attempt can succeed. You and I are "psychosomatic organisms," as modern medical science would say. We do not *have* bodies, as if these were garments to be put on or taken off, but *are* bodies. We are also minds; we do not *have* them, either. So it is that we must accept ourselves for what we are. The implications of this fact are enormous, for they have consequences in respect to our way of living, our way of relating to others, and our way of understanding our desires, urges, yearnings, mistakes, and triumphs.

In the fourth place, we belong with our fellow humans. We should not be able to develop our capacity to understand ourselves unless we had others around us and with us. Anybody who has watched a baby grow into childhood knows that it is through awareness of others that the process takes place. First the baby becomes conscious of the others who care for it, who supply its needs; and then, and as a consequence, the baby begins to see that it is a self, a self who lives with its family and who needs them not only for its security but also for its ability to be healthy and to grow into maturity. What is thus true of babies as they move toward adulthood is true, in its own way, of the whole of our human existence. Proud assertion of *my* self is disastrous, for it can cut me off from the others whom I need. Healthy growth depends always upon acceptance of those others, with whom we live and in sensitive relationship with whom we begin to live well.

The fifth point to stress is the rationality which makes us different from the animals. Although we may not be able to think very well, none the less we *do* think. Humans are "reasoning animals." We take this for granted; but we should add that humans are also able *to will*—that is, to direct effort toward the accomplishment of what seems good and right to us. We also have "feeling-tones," as William James put it, deep appreciative, evaluational, or sensitive capacity. We like and we dislike, we esteem or we do not esteem, we appreciate or we do not appreciate, this and that. The Greeks spoke of this as the "aesthetic" quality; they did not mean by that adjective "pretty things" or even beauty in terms of artistic experience, although that was included. The word "aesthetic" had for them a wider significance, embracing the whole feeling-capacity which marks human existence.

A corollary of this ability to feel deeply is found in our sixth stress: the human capacity to love and to receive love from others. As we have already insisted, human life at its best and finest, in the "peak experiences" which give importance to our whole existence, is known when we are "in love." Loving means openness to others, entering into communion with them, sharing their lives, receiving from them what they would give us of themselves, and finding through this experience a joy and fulfillment nowhere else obtainable. Beyond this, Christians would dare to claim that such love is the end for which we are being made; thus, to live "in love" is to be on the way to becoming truly human and it is the movement of human existence toward the "image of God." In Jesus Christ human love is adequately and decisively expressed and for that reason he can be, what Christian faith has always declared him to be, the embodiment or "incarnation" of God, the cosmic Love, the cosmic Lover.

Humanity's ability to learn to love and to accept love leads us to the seventh human characteristic. This has to do with the implicit awareness of the reality of God. Obviously most of the time this is not clear, precise, or vividly conscious; indeed most of the time it is not articulated at all. But what I am getting at here is the sensitivity of people to the pressure of love upon them, their recognition that it is indeed "what makes the world go round," and their yearning to live in love and both to give and receive love. We do not need to think or talk in esoteric language when we speak of God. God is a mysterious reality, to be sure; no human mind can comprehend God, for God's infinity or inexhaustibility is beyond that comprehension. At the same time, God leaves traces (Augustine spoke in Latin of *vestigia*) of himself, so that his children may never lose contact with him. The traces are precisely those yearnings, desires, strivings, which may be summed up in the simple word "love," once we have removed the sentimental, cheap, and easy connotations which so often are attached to it. The "witness to God in the human soul," as devotional writers have styled it, is this sense of significance or importance given when we realize our capacity for, and our need of, love as the fulfillment of our finite and limited human existence. What is more, love always has about it the quality of "everlastingness"; the boy or girl who says to another, "I love you," is also saying *sotto voce,* "for ever and ever." This may be a delusion, in our human finitude; but the reality of that everlastingness is none the less something that we all sense. An evidence of this is found when we hear people saying that once "the right person comes along" the love will be "for keeps, for always." Thus in this intimation of divine Love present in human loving there is a guarantee that humans are being made for something greater and more all-inclusive than creaturely existence. Augustine put this in words that have become famous, words which he addressed to God as he began his own life-story in *The Confessions:* "Thou hast made us to move toward thee, O God, and our hearts are in disquietude unless and until they find their fulfillment in thee."

Finally, and as the eighth of our points, men and women have genuine freedom to make significant decisions, decisions which have consequences that they know they must responsibly accept and for which they feel accountable. However limited this freedom may be for various reasons, nevertheless there *is* this freedom, of which all of us are conscious. Indeed decision, in an analogous fashion, runs through the whole cosmos, although this is not obvious at the levels of non-conscious existence.

Furthermore, our decisions have their results. The world goes on by such decisions made and by such results following. At the human level, you and I are affected by our past, in terms of which we decide what to do about present possibilities, and toward the making real of some goal or end which to us seems good and proper. The basic question in human life is whether these decisions are truly toward, or away from, *genuine* fulfillment, which is to say whether or not they move us in the direction of loving, living in love, sharing in love.

I have tried to outline, in eight brief points, what it means to be human. Though they may seem abstract, I am sure that if you and I take these eight points and think about them, we shall see that they *do* indicate what we are as men and women. We are dynamic, dependent, social, rational and willing and feeling, capable of loving and of receiving love; we are implicitly aware of the demands made by (and help provided from) a Love which is greater than our own poor and inadequate sample, and able to decide in some considerable freedom for or against living as loving, caring, concerned persons. This, I believe, is what a Christian would want to say about human nature; and it is derived from the total scriptural picture and the concrete known experience of each of us.

But now there comes the tragic fact that we humans are also very defective in our making actual that which we truly *are*. The late Dr. Harry Emerson Fosdick, a noted preacher of the last generation, used to repeat that the demand addressed to us is, "Become what you are." "Become"—that is, make real and actual—"what you are"—that is, the intention or purpose of your humanity. The sad truth is that we decline to do just that. Here is the significance of the religious conception of "sin."

For many, sin is a matter of disobeying rules laid down once for all by God, perhaps in some pronouncement from on high such as the giving of the Ten Commandments. But to think in that way is mistaken. Sin is primarily human failure to become what it is in us to be, "to become what we are"; and since it is God's will for us that we should thus become truly human, to fail in this respect, and to fail by our own decisions, is also a violation of the divine purpose for us. This is a much more serious defect than the mere violation of particular regulations, mostly negative, which are laid down in inherited codes of ethics. And the Ten Commandments, along with the deliverances of the "natural moral law"—that we "should avoid evil and do the good," as Thomas Aquinas summed up that law—are the traditional ways in which either negatively or positively this deep failure to become human may be understood, at some given time and in some particular place. When "lists of sins" do not point us in that direction, they are utterly wrong. When they do, they can help us to see our possible fulfillment and the many ways in which, by this or that decision and by our acting upon the choice made, we are rejecting our potentiality as children of God, in our failure to live "in love and charity" with our neighbors, in and under the Love which is God.

The consequence of decisions which are *against* that cosmic drive or thrust is an alienation of human existence from its true fulfillment. Thus we are estranged from our real selves, as God intends them to be; we are estranged from our fellow humans, with whom we should be living in concord and understanding, with justice and sympathy; we are estranged from the world itself, regarding it as our possession which we can use as we please and hence damage almost, if not entirely, beyond repair; and above all, we are estranged from God who is making us "toward himself" and everywhere and always invites, lures, solicits, and encourages us to respond lovingly, so far as we are able, to the chance of loving—and hence of *living* in a fully human way.

Emphasis upon this willed defection in human life is part of the Christian understanding of what it means to be human. Sometimes the emphasis has been made in an extreme fashion, so that man is regarded as a "mass of corruption" with no possibility of extrication from the mess into which he has got himself. Certainly the long accumulation of human decisions through many millennia has made it practically impossible for any human being to move forward without help—and to move forward in the *right* direction: this is the meaning of the old doctrine of "original sin," however much that meaning has been distorted by confusing it with human sexuality, a confusion we owe, unfortunately, to the same Augustine who more often spoke beautifully and christianly of divine Love and human loving. On the other hand, the central assertion of Christian faith, indeed the gospel itself, is that God *has* made available his help, a way out of this appalling dilemma.

Years ago, in one of my first books, I put this in these words: "To man in his need, God comes with his deed." I believe this still holds true. Humans *are* in need of "salvation," of being made healthy and whole. The gospel proclaims, as we shall emphasize in the next chapter, that God *acts,* above all acts in Jesus Christ, and that in this activity of God, through his loving identification with humankind, wholeness and health are provided, if only we are prepared humbly to accept what is offered to us. This is what the traditional doctrine of the "Atonement" is talking about. This is "the benefit of Christ," as an older theology used to say—it is Christ's "work"; and it is this which gives point to our speaking about his "person."

God's activity for and with and in human persons is a persuasive, loving activity; it is not primarily an exercise of power in any coercive sense. The one thing that such coercive power does is to prevent things from going completely awry. God exercises such coercion solely with the aim of avoiding chaos and anarchy in the world and in human life; thus, God sets the limits of possible defection on the part of creatures. But in his "proper work," as Luther said, God is always gracious—always "Love-in-action." God loves his world and he loves his human children; he works lovingly to bring them to himself, to receive them into his own divine loving, and thus to fulfil and to complete the hints and intimations of love he has put in their hearts.

IV
Christ

The worshipful and loving One whom we call God is always and everywhere related to the world, always and everywhere active in it, and always and everywhere self-identified with it through care and concern for the creation. This is the "general truth," as we may call it, which Christianity asserts. But general truths, in whatever area of discourse, do not have much cutting-edge; they do not make much appeal since they are not sufficiently vivid and decisive to awaken a heartfelt commitment. This is a plain fact of experience.

Suppose someone tells a friend, "All politicians are likely to be open to influence of the sort that produces corruption." The friend, though probably quite willing to believe what has been said, is almost certain to say something like this, "Yes, that's probably the case, but let's consider an instance." In other words, general statements need to be illustrated by one or more decisive events. "All the world loves a lover," it is said. As true as that may well be, it can never come alive to us until and unless we see some instance of a response made to this or that special case where a lover *is* loved.

So we may say, God does indeed care for and love this world, acting in it faithfully and unfailingly; but only as and when we see some place or point where this is vividly and vitally expressed in concrete event or happening can we accept it with all our hearts and respond to it with joy and then act in accordance with what it has to tell us.

Now I have just put in a very simple way something that theology expresses precisely in technical language when it speaks about *general* revelation and *special* revelation. In many different ways God is active, and hence truly revealed, in the affairs of humankind and in the going-on of the world. But in the Man Jesus—with all that happened to give sense to his life, with the things he himself said and did, with the way in which he was received, with the consequences of his coming—Christians declare that God is *specially* revealed.

Sometimes people have thought that they rightly exalt Jesus when they make him entirely different from anything and everything else. He is taken to be "unique" in the sense that there is nothing else, anywhere in our experience, which can be seen as parallel in any degree to his life of love in action. But we do not rightly exalt Jesus when we make him simply unintelligible. As Aristotle saw centuries ago, something which is absolutely unique is absolutely unintelligible; we can make no sense of it. In a variety of ways, of which historians of Christian thought are aware, the great Christian thinkers have always tried to preserve the *once-ness* of Jesus, or his speciality (and I use that word in its British, not its American sense, seeking by it to indicate a quality of decisiveness and particularity); at the same time, they have always found some way to relate him to the rest of what God is up to and what God is doing in the world.

Perhaps still another approach to this matter may be helpful. A number of contemporary Christian theologians have been prepared to follow the view suggested by Whitehead and by Charles Hartshorne. From this Process viewpoint, God's relationship to the world is like the relationship of the mind to the body which the mind "informs" and by which it expresses itself. This is not panthe-

ism, which identifies God with the world; it is pan*en*the-
ism, which means that while God and the world are distinct one from the other, they are yet interrelated and
never entirely separated one from the other. You cannot
locate your mind in any particular part of your total organism, yet it is operative in every part of that organism.

Nor is this view strange to Christian thought in its traditional sense. When a questioner has said to me that it *is*
strange, I have liked to quote some words from the great
medieval Christian theologian Thomas Aquinas (than
whom nobody could be more orthodox!): "In his rule God
stands in relation to the whole universe as the soul stands
in relation to the body" *(II Sent. dist. 1, q. 1, ad 1).* From
the very man who, in Roman Catholic theology, has been
taken as *the* teacher of orthodox Christian faith we have
words which help us enormously to understand, from a
human analogy that we can all grasp, how God and his
world are related one with the other.

Yet here once again we must notice that while it is
indeed true that our mind (Aquinas uses the word "soul,"
but he means the same thing) is unfailingly related to our
body during our lifetime and is always actively at work in
that body, there are occasions, times, moments, when that
relation and that working are more vividly recognized for
what they are. When with full conscious decision I determine to do *this*, not *that,* my mind is plainly and obviously
seen as active. Above all, most of us would wish to say,
when somebody gives himself or herself utterly to another, in love and mutual care, we grasp better than elsewhere the reality of the mind or soul, personhood in its
most complete reality, wonderfully exerting its influence
and showing its strength. Thus, if God is like the mind at
work in the body, so far as God's relationship with and
activity in the world are concerned, then the deity is
decisively related with and active in the world at that
point and in that place where there is a full and generous

giving on God's part and an open and adequate response
on man's part. For Christian faith, this point and place are
the total event which we name when we say *Jesus Christ.*

In the long story of the Jewish people, we learn that in
the first days of their tribal existence, they were so over-
whelmed by the release of sheer power in the natural
world—in storm, thunder, earthquake, and the like—that
they "modeled" the God whom they worshiped after the
pattern of just such release of power. He was the entirely
omnipotent and all-controlling force in the world. Soon
they saw him also operative in their own warfare with
alien and oppressive neighbors. He was the "Lord of
hosts," the God of battle who was with them as their
strong defender and helper.

Presently, however, under the influence of men like
Moses, the early Jews came to see that God's power was
not sheer force; on the contrary, it was "the power that
makes for righteousness," to use a phrase of the Victorian
essayist Matthew Arnold. This righteousness was to be
manifested in their own Jewish society, because God re-
quired it of his children; it was also to be shown in their
relations with other people, more particularly "the stran-
ger [foreigner] within their gates." Nor did the movement toward deeper understanding of God's character
stop there—although, unhappily, many people who think
themselves Christian seem often to assume that it did and
therefore look upon God as powerful and righteous, but
as little else. Under the great prophets, from Hosea on
down to men like Jeremiah, the experience of those who
turned to God and sought to know him as they responded
to the events in their lives and in their history led them
to see that the righteousness of God was marked by what
they styled *hesed,* a Hebrew word which means "lovingkindness" or "mercy." God was *not* primarily the all-pow-
erful one, neither was he primarily the one who de-
manded righteousness or justice from his children. Above

all he was a God of mercy or lovingkindness. His power as well as his righteousness therefore must be interpreted precisely in terms of that mercy and lovingkindness. This insight, awakened as a response to that which God was believed to have done and to be doing, comes to its highest expression in the so-called Suffering Servant poems of Isaiah, which speak of one who so identifies himself with others that he suffers for them, shares in their anguish and distress, and yet is able to "see of the travail of his soul and be satisfied"—that is, conquer the evil in the world and emerge victorious and triumphant, not by the use of force but by the exercise of loving concern.

When Jesus came, he accepted this teaching of his Jewish ancestors but he also did more. He taught that God's loving concern is not only such that he will gladly receive those who turn to him, but is also (and much more importantly) itself outgoing, seeking, striving to awaken the response of his children. In his teaching Jesus talked about this continually. And in what he *did,* he demonstrated it in action. He went out to seek and find "the lost"; he himself was like the shepherd who seeks the lost sheep, the woman who looks diligently for the lost coin, the loving father who runs to embrace the son who has left home and is afraid (yet desirous) of returning.

Even more significant, however, is the fact that looking back on the whole life of Jesus, after his death and the wonderful sense of his renewed presence and power which we call "the event of the resurrection," the first Christian believers came to see that what Jesus taught and did was what Jesus himself really *was.* In him, in his teaching and doing and in the totality of his personality and what it had brought about in the lives of men, the loving concern of God was operating, decisively and vividly and definitively and crucially. Once the first Christians grasped this astonishing reality—or better, found themselves grasped by it so that they could not help but re-

spond in commitment and discipleship—they were able
to say, "In *him* God has visited and redeemed his people."
They put it in many different ways, such as "In Christ God
was reconciling men to himself," or "In this was manifested the love of God, that he sent his Son," or (in the grand
phrases of John's Gospel), in Jesus "the Word [God's activity in self-expression and self-giving] was made flesh [was
embodied in a genuine human life], and dwelt among
us, . . ." (1:14).

Thus we can see that because of their Jewish background and because of what had happened to them in
Jesus Christ, Christians from the beginning were prepared to make exalted claims about their Lord. When
they were in touch with *him,* God was in touch with *them.*
By and through the humanity which he wore as a royal
vesture, they declared, God had drawn near as never
before and as nowhere else. And he had done this in one
of their own kind, in a real Man whom their "hands had
handled" and whom they had seen and known "in the
flesh."

What we have here is an affirmation that somehow or
other in this Jesus God and man were united in a very
special way. Not that this denied God's other and various
acts of self-disclosure. Rather, it both confirmed and com-
plemented them *and* corrected mistakes and inadequacies in interpreting what had gone before. There were
four significant matters which were included in this response of faith; and the rest of this chapter will be devoted
to a consideration of them: (1) *God* is genuinely and actually active in this Jesus; (2) the activity of God is in true and
real human terms, since Jesus is a *Man;* (3) in him God and
man are brought together in *personal unity;* and (4) as a
result of this unity, God's other children may enter upon
a relationship in which *they too share in the sonship to
God seen in Christ:* they are *filii in Filio* ("sons in the

Son"), as the Christian Fathers of the first centuries of our
era liked to phrase it. These four points are the meaning
of the traditional Christian doctrines of "Incarnation" and
"Atonement."

First, God is active in the total human existence of Jesus.
The presence and the activity of God has been felt in
many ways, at many times, and in many places. People
may not have *called* what they felt by that name, which
after all is simply a human invention and in itself, as a
word, has no special holiness. But whatever they may
have called it, men and women have known themselves
uplifted by some splendid piece of music, a great work of
art, a beautiful landscape. They have sensed in the call of
duty and in the responsible exercise of that duty more
than merely human instinct or wish. They have glimpsed
truth which made inexorable demands upon them, so that
they would rather be killed than deny that truth. They
have been ready to go to death for some principle or value
which they believed to be absolutely supreme. And they
have felt themselves enriched and their lives made
worthwhile through "falling in love" and finding that
their love is an answer to a love that calls for response.

These are some of the ways in which what we might
well call "ultimacy" has become for men and women a
matter of what we might with equal appropriateness call
"immediacy." It comes down to the plain truth that people have sensed and still do sense a significance to their
existence which they may deny in word but cannot contradict in fact. They know that there is an "importance,"
as I like to phrase it, about human existence; and they
know that they did not create, entirely out of their own
fantasy, the importance that they believe does attach to
living. This explains, of course, why for most of us suicide
seems a disloyal and immoral act; it also explains why
even persons who take their own lives somehow believe

that by doing so they can assert the importance or significance which other persons or circumstances beyond their
control appear to negate or deny.

An English theologian, Dr. H. H. Farmer, has called this
widely diffused experience a feeling of help or succor in
difficulty and a demand made upon us that we live life as
best we can; he says that this is a kind of hidden presence
of God in the world. The trouble is that it is all too vague
and too indeterminate. What people need is something
that speaks to them compellingly and with clarity, which
requires of them an answer, whether that answer be a yes
or a no.

From the very beginning to the present, Christians
have found that they meet in Jesus precisely such demand
and help; they have discovered that when they relate
themselves to him, in a dedication or engagement of their
lives, they are given a point for living, a significant meaning for existence, an awareness of the importance that
redeems them from triviality and frustration. So they
have said that *God* is there.

But at the same time they have recognized that our
second point is also true. The God whom they meet in
Jesus is brought near to them in one of their own kind, in
a fellow *Man*. The genuine historical humanity of Jesus,
about which the gospel stories tell us, has been just as real
as the sense that in him God is to be discovered making
himself known. This is why any attempt to minimize or
deny the humanity of Jesus is fatal to Christian faith. And
it is interesting to notice that whereas today it is the *divinity* found in Jesus that may cause problems for some people, it was the *humanity* of Jesus that in the early days of
the Church had to be vigorously asserted against those
who thought they were doing him service by saying that
it was only his divinity, or the divinity working through
him, that mattered.

There have always been people who distrust the world

and hence sneer at the humanity which all of us share. They would like to be "as the angels," who in classical theological definition are "incorporeal spirits"; they find distasteful the flesh and blood which is ours, the bodily instincts and desires which we know so well, and the necessity for our dragging about with us (as they think) the "bodiness" which Shakespeare once styled "this muddy vesture of decay." The Christian Church, at its best and in its official teaching, has never taken this attitude. It has found the world a good creation of God, however wrong things may be in it. Christians have valued human existence, even when that includes defection or sin. They have dared to believe that sex, which those anti-body people so dislike, is a good and wonderful thing because it is both a creation of God and the necessary ground or condition for our growing into human lovers, however distorted and twisted some sexual behavior may be. They have been ready to say that Jesus was "made of the dust of the earth," like the rest of us; that he shared human anguish as well as human joy; and that in every respect he was "like unto us"—save in one respect, namely that he used all his human characteristics and qualities in the right (that is, the God-intended and humanly fulfilling) fashion and hence was "without sin."

If Jesus was thus genuinely human, he must have shared the limitations which are inevitable for humanity. He did not know all there was to know and what he did know he knew as a Jew of the first century. He knew bodily pain and he knew bodily joy; he knew also the temptations which human existence involves and the ease with which the less good paths may be chosen—although he was able, in his own way and at the cost of great anguish, to choose the truly good road. In his thinking he was naturally influenced by the patterns of belief which he inherited, even if he selected from those patterns the central things and rejected the peripheral and ephemeral ones.

We need never be afraid that by stressing to the full this real humanity of Jesus we shall do damage to the divinity which worked in him. Nor need we fear that when we discover (as we have lately done) that much of his attitude to God and the world has parallels in other teaching, as for example that of the Essenes whose Dead Sea Scrolls have lately been recovered, we have thereby denied to him his special place in Christian faith. No, for Jesus is genuinely and truly a Man.

God at work in him; humanity at its best in him: these two are together in his life in a personal unity which is unshakeable and secure. That is the third of the four big claims which the Christian wishes to make about Jesus in order to remain faithful to the age-old belief of Christian history.

We must ask, therefore, *how* such a personal unity could be established in that Man, at that time and place. The answer, I suggest, must take very seriously the priority of the divine Love and Lover for all our human loving; and along with that, the responsive character of this human loving. The difficulty has arisen, for the most part, when Christians have talked about God and man as if these two were *things*—"substances," almost modeled after material entities like fire and water. Or it has come when God has been seen as essentially a coercive power and human freedom as practically non-existent. In each of these instances, it is very hard to see how there can be a genuine human, let alone a truly personal, analogy for God and Man united in Christ. On the other hand, if we think of God as the cosmic Lover and define the cosmic thrust or drive as nothing other than such "pure unbounded Love," and at the same time think of humankind as being created to become a reflection and expression of that Love, we can begin to see how there can be a genuine, fully human, fully divine, and truly personal unity of the two.

I am convinced that we shall make sense of the ancient belief in the Incarnation if we begin by seeing the whole world as the sphere of God's incarnating activity, with time providing the *when* and space the *where* for that loving movement of God. Then we can go on to say that God as Love, while always and everywhere active, can and does act with a special intensity in particular places. *The* place of this action with an intensity beyond all human understanding is in the total human existence of a Galilean artisan who was ready, thanks to the long preparatory stages in Jewish history, to respond in human loving and with filial obedience to the divine Lover reaching out to humankind. Two Greek words, used by some of the theologians of the ancient school of Antioch, are to the point here: *eudokia* and *sunapheia*. The former signifies God's "good pleasure" in seeking out and finding, but also in preparing and establishing, a humanity which would be God's own agency for expressing the innermost heart of Love. The latter signifies a unity established by prevenient divine act and responding human act—a unity which is truly personal.

Last of all, our fourth stress, the unity which God and Man achieved in Jesus—which was "determined, dared, and done" in him, to use Christopher Smart's splendid words from *The Song of David*—has its consequences throughout creation. The unity there given is a unity into which others may enter; it is not confined to Jesus Christ alone, although it originates in him. Atonement is a word which can be broken down, as many have pointed out, into three one syllable words: "at-one-ment." To be "at one" with God is to overcome the alienation and estrangement which men and women know so well, which separates them from their true selves, from their fellows, from the world, and from God. But thus to be "at one" is to be reconciled and redeemed. It is to be "saved," as the old hymns tell us, from our state of sin; which is to say, to be put on the right path, restored from our deviation and distortion of direction, and given a new start.

Many symbols have been used in Christian thought and devotion to state this enduring experience of Christian people. Some have spoken of the overcoming of the evil powers or demons which stand between God and us; others have talked about deliverance from imprisonment and the freedom of genuine sons who no longer are treated as slaves; still others have told of the injection of healthy immortal life which cures men and women from the disease and corruption which they experience apart from God. But all these are *symbols,* each of them useful at this or that time and in the light of this or that cultural milieu. The reality to which the symbols point is just one thing: it is a unity of life, on the way to full integration, where men and women are so related to what I have styled the cosmic thrust or drive, God himself, that they can go on bravely and fearlessly toward "the mark of their high calling." And what is that? Nothing other than increasing conformity to Jesus Christ himself, who is the very image of God, the one in whom divine Loving was operative with incredible speciality in a human loving which wins us and enables us to move forward as those who have become "sons in *the* Son."

V
The Holy Spirit

Until quite recently the Holy Spirit has been, as someone facetiously put it, "the forgotten man in the Godhead." Hymns have ended with a verse in which the Spirit has been mentioned, along with the Father and the Son, in a kind of postscript addressed to the Trinity. At ordinations and on other special occasions the ancient "Come Holy Ghost, our souls inspire" has been sung. Once a year on the Feast of Pentecost (or Whitsunday) something may have been said in sermons on the Spirit. But for the most part the Holy Spirit has played little part in the thought of the ordinary Christian.

Nowadays all that is changed. The so-called "Pentecostal sects" and "charismatic groups" have been in the news. We have heard about "speaking with tongues in the Spirit"; and we have all come to know a little about what enthusiasts called "the birth in the Spirit" as given to at first a few, and now an increasing number, of men and women of varying ages who tell us that nobody can really claim the Christian name unless there has been some such experience in addition to the formal ecclesiastical rite of confirmation or its equivalent.

As a matter of fact, thinkers within the Church throughout the centuries have been a bit puzzled about just "what to do" with the Spirit. Their formal inclusion of the Spirit in the doctrine of God has seemed only to succeed in complicating considerably what is said about deity. But as one of my own teachers used to say, the Holy Spirit has never been the object of a "cult" or a special devotion and has usually been mentioned as a kind of afterthought in theological formulations. As we have indicated, however, all this has now changed.

So it is not irrelevant for us to devote a chapter in this book on theology for the layperson to the Holy Spirit. Nor is it improper to conclude the chapter, as we shall do, with some discussion of the triunitarian view of God which introduction of the Spirit, in addition to the Father and the Son, makes necessary. Perhaps a discussion of the Triunity—I prefer this term to the usual word *Trinity,* for reasons which will appear in the following—may seem like engaging in high speculation, rather than attempting (as we have sought to do) to keep down to earth by dealing only with matters that are primary and essential in the life of the Christian disciple. I believe otherwise; and I am convinced that any model of God which is faithful both to the main emphases in the faith we inherit and to the deliverances of genuine discipleship must necessarily engage us in just such a triunitarian way of thinking about the deepest cosmic thrust which we name when we use the word God.

In trying to understand the significance of the Holy Spirit, we shall do well to begin by noting that it is a common mode of speech to talk about people's being "inspired" or about their having some sort of "inspiration." What is here said has to do with awareness of an empowering or enhancing of ordinary human powers of thought and action by that which is greater than anything normally found in that human exercise. To be inspired, or to be conscious of inspiration, is to have the sense that our human capacities can be, and sometimes are, enhanced to such a degree and in such a way that we almost feel ourselves to be taken in charge by a reality not our own.

Great poets and artists, great musicians, people who are creative in one or another area, are often said to be thus inspired.

Now when we look at the words we are using here, we can readily recognize that one of their ingredients is precisely "spirit," with a lowercase *s*. I am fond of quoting a saying of the novelist D. H. Lawrence who in a poem claimed that what he wrote was not written so much *by him* as "by the wind that blows through me." The word "wind" is nothing but an English synonym for "spirit"; and what Lawrence is telling us is that he believed, rightly or wrongly, that his writing was not merely the exercise of his own imagination in all its finitude but was more certainly a mode of expression which was given to him from beyond and above his own powers.

Furthermore, everybody knows what is meant when we speak of "the spirit" of a school or of a nation or of a team or of an age in history. Here we seem very much down to earth, since what we are getting at in using those phrases is the very real experience of sharing in a common life which has a quality greater than the day-by-day routine or practice, so much greater indeed that those who share in that life, whether in a team or a school or a nation or elsewhere, are grasped by it and identify themselves in terms of it. Thus "the spirit" of a school is an intangible reality, yet a very real one, for anybody who has entered at all deeply into the life of the institution and been "caught up" into a pervasive if ill-defined *something* which constitutes what we mean when we name that school.

If we look back to the first days of Christian faith as reflected in the New Testament writings we can see that exactly this was the experience of the disciples after Jesus' death and renewed presence among them. They felt compelled to respond in dedication of self to the risen Lord, not merely by their own admiration of that Lord but more

significantly by something very much like the spirit of a
school—in this case, the spirit which animated and moved
through the Christian community. Once Jesus had come
and taught and acted, had died and had risen, there was
an answer to be given, a response to be made. The key
word here is "response." The first Christians made it. The
response which they made, as they turned to the memory
of the Jesus they had known and as they experienced the
renewed power which came from him after he had been
taken from their sight, was so vigorous, so strong and
impelling, but withal so entirely a personalizing affair,
that they could only use of it the traditional ancient Jewish
phrases about *God's* Spirit at work in them.

They remembered the prophecies of the Jewish seers,
notably that of Joel who had spoken of a future outpouring
of God's Spirit; and with this in mind they were quick to
claim that they themselves were indeed experiencing the
working of God in their midst—but of God acting in a
mode or fashion other than that which they had witnessed
in Jesus himself. The powers they experienced in their
response to Jesus, crucified yet still alive in their own lives,
was "inspiring;" it gave them "inspiration," a sense of
more than the purely and solely human. So they spoke of
this response as "in the Spirit"; and they were sure that
God was truly at work in that response.

Sometimes this experience was so exciting that those
who had it were taken "out of themselves" and began to
speak in words which had no ordinary meaning but were
an outflowing of deep internal pressures—this is the
"speaking with tongues" which in some circles has reap-
peared in our own time. Usually, the experience was such
that "enthusiasm"—the word itself means, in its original
usage, "possessed by a spirit"—marked their meetings
and they felt themselves strangely uplifted and emotionally thrilled by their faith. Even more often the experience expressed itself in a certain quality of life about

which Paul wrote when he described "the harvest of the Spirit": love, joy, peace, long-suffering, meekness, moderation, self-control (Galatians 5:22).

Occasionally the sense of the Spirit's presence and work led this or that individual to make claims for himself, or to act by himself, without much regard for the Christian community as a whole. But the more frequent result of the Spirit was a deepening and enriching of the community itself, so that the sharing of life as Christians became both the goal sought and the experience known.

Finally, as Christian thought began to work out some coherent statement of what faith and life in the community implied, the assertion was made that *all response* to God, not least in the various rites and ceremonies of the community itself (such as entrance into it by Baptism and the receiving in the Lord's Supper of "the spiritual food" of Christ's own life) was done "in the Spirit"; and through the empowering activity of that Spirit which took "of the things of Christ" and made them come alive in the common worship, the discipleship, and the discipline which marked the Christian society out from the rest of the culture in which it had its setting.

If response is the first key word to our understanding of the significance of Christian inspiration, the second key word is precisely the *enthusiasm* to which we have just referred. Enthusiasm need not be violent and emotionally heated. Most of us know a quiet sort of enthusiastic interest in some person or cause which has secured our response, quite as much as others share the more obvious and visible enthusiasm which in some people is their natural way of expressing themselves. Human psychology and physiology play their part here. "It takes all sorts to make the world"; one sort of person has the constitutional equipment, as we might call it, which brings him to shout or sing or dance; another sort has a different make-up and is more likely to show the enthusiasm he feels in less

obvious ways. A great writer of the first decades of this
century, the Anglo-German Friedrich von Hügel, was ac-
customed to speak of different *attraits*—ways of being
drawn—toward God; we can profit by that recognition
and accept the plain fact that there are many and various
modes for the human expression of the desire of men and
women to respond to what they know of God and of God's
activity in the world.

In this connection, it is important to notice that the
great contribution of the "Spirit movements" of our day,
like the Pentecostalists and charismatics, is in their having
made it imperative for *all* of us to take with great seriousness the reality of the Spirit. The particular sorts of expression which they find appropriate and inevitable need not
be adopted by everybody, for that would be a failure to
recognize what Paul called "diversities of gifts" and what
we have just referred to by speaking of differing psycho-
logical-physiological make-up. At the same time, the insistence on the fact and place of the Spirit in the life of the
Christian community does need reemphasis; and we may
be grateful to those movements for just this renewed
stress.

Now we may turn to a consideration of what the Spirit
does—by which I mean the ways in which, within the life
both of the Church *and* of the Christian believer, the
Spirit operates to bring us toward God as he declares
himself in the life of Jesus Christ and in the ongoing Christian witness down through the ages. And I believe that
these may be summed up in four words: The Spirit *in-
forms* Church and Christian, so that both may be conformed to Christ; the Spirit *inspires* or enlivens the
Church and the Christian; the Spirit *discloses* new aspects
or facets of that which God in Christ has done; and the
Spirit *enables* the Church and the Christian to show
deeper and more demanding fidelity to that which they
believe.

In the first place, then, the Holy Spirit *informs* those who are drawn to respond to God in Christ. That includes you and me. But by *inform* I do not suggest that the Spirit tells us something; I mean, rather, that he in-forms the Christian and the Christian Church, giving them a capacity to answer the one whom both adore. The purpose of that *in*-forming is to *conform*—and I do not apologize for this play on words—to the quality of life, the love-in-action, which is found in the Lord and which indeed is Jesus' own response to the divine Love that spoke to him, worked in him, and moved through him. The whole business of Christian discipleship, for each professing and practicing Christian, is a process of growing conformity to the Lord. Thus William Law, the English divine of an earlier day known to us through his remarkable writing on spirituality, could speak of the life of the ordinary believer as "the process of Christ" working itself out in the believer. So also the Christian community, in its corporate response and through its worship and sacramental acts, is in process of being thus conformed, by the Spirit, to the Lord in whom it sees the action of God for human wholeness.

In the second place, the Spirit *inspires.* He enlivens and strengthens the yearning of the believer, and the corporate existence of the Christian Church too, to reflect in word and deed the same quality of life in love, with its many different forms of expression, which in Jesus Christ has been demonstrated at an historical moment. Inspiration is not a mechanical affair; and we do the notion of inspiration grave injustice when we talk about it as if it were a matter of God's coercing or forcing people, either personally or in their social relationships. On the contrary, as always God acts in human existence by invitation, lure, solicitation, and the sheer attraction that the beloved has for the lover. Here is personal relationship of the highest order. Often it is invisible; usually it is "anonymous," in the sense that its primary concern is not to point to itself but to point toward the one who is loved. This is why in Christian devotion, as the tradition has it, we pray "in" the Spirit, rather than "to" the Spirit; and it is worth noticing that for the most part the prayers which we inherit and which have been translated into English for our prayer books are not directed to the Spirit but to the Father, through the "mediation" (or by the expression of God toward us) of the Son, while the Spirit is usually spoken of as the mode of the divine being which makes such praying possible at all. As Paul tells us, the Spirit himself "prays in us," which is a way of affirming that our feeble efforts at intimate relationship with God are inspired, enlivened, made real and vital, by that Spirit.

Thirdly, the Spirit *discloses* new aspects or facets of God's character and action, taking (John's Gospel puts it) "of the things of Christ and declaring them unto us." In his teaching, as well as in his concrete doings, Jesus exhibited God's ways with us and his purposes for us. But no single human existence, not even that of Christ himself, could conceivably exhaust the riches of God's working. Hence we need to learn how to apply what we have received to other and different circumstances; we need also to be given a clue or key so that the new knowledge which is ours may be tested by the criterion of its christlikeness. Whatever is in accordance with Christ's whole character and the Spirit in him is "of Christ." Whatever is not thus in accordance is *not* "of Christ." And the Spirit, who is the same Spirit given to Christ "without measure," works in appropriate degree and manner to open our eyes to discern the how and the where of God's present working in the world.

Then, as a fourth point, the Spirit *enables* the loyalty or fidelity which marks the Christian's discipleship. Each of us is weak in our response, incompetent in our discernment, inadequate in our effort to act out our Christian profession, as we know very well. Each of us therefore needs, and by the Spirit is given, the enabling power to continue or, as the old writers used to say, to "persevere." Each of us needs, and by the Spirit is given, the courage to stand fast in this profession of ours, so that in moments of doubt and hesitation, as well as in our failure in and loss of faith, we may begin once again and go on in the Christian life. This help the Spirit provides. Thus it comes to pass that the entire business of Christian living, once we have accepted the wonderful reality of God's acceptance of us, is "sanctification"—"being made holy" by being enabled more and more to let "the new Adam" grow in us and replace the "old Adam," which was our willingness to rest content with the deviations and distortions that spring from wrong self-centeredness, pride, and wanting to have our own way regardless of God or of our fellows.

We can see, therefore, that the Holy Spirit is of enormous importance as a matter of practical Christian experience. A theology of the Spirit is no added speculation which only complicates matters for us. Far from it; the Holy Spirit is the most real and vital of all our ways of knowing and experiencing God himself. But of course the Spirit is not often obvious in this; as we have intimated, he points toward God in Christ, not to himself. One of my teachers called the Spirit "the humblest person of the Godhead"; he was making exactly that same point about the way in which the Spirit moves us in the direction of God's image in Christ and will not let us rest content until we have started to move toward that image.

However in full-orbed Christian thinking, the Holy Spirit is not considered to be restricted to Christian experience, but is present and at work everywhere. In any time or at any place where something of God has been disclosed, under whatever incognitos this may be, there is some sort of answering-back, some sort of response. There is some degree, maybe very slight indeed, of in-forming, inspiring, disclosing, and enabling. This may be in a quite "secular" fashion, where we should never think of *naming* what is going on as "divine." None the less, in any and every response to goodness lived out, truth shown, beauty made visible, justice manifested, and love expressed, the Holy Spirit is at work. The cosmic dimension of the Spirit's operation cannot be forgotten, just because the place where we know him best is in the intimacy and ultimacy of Christian life in Christ.

And this brings us to the doctrine of the Trinity—or, as I prefer, Triunity of God. This term refers to the whole reality of God's working in the world and hence for the whole reality of God himself. God is not a bare unity, as if he were like a human individual without relationships, standing quite alone. God is always in relationship; as we have said before, relationship and love are almost identical in meaning, provided the relationship is deep, sincere, and all-embracing. God is not a simple monad, as they used to say; rather, he is richly a relationship in himself, love going forth and being answered by love, and the love which unites the going-out and the answering-back is itself nothing other than love-acting. So Augustine dared once to phrase it, when he was seeking some analogy from human experience to apply to the God whom he was describing for his readers.

From the super-abundance of the divine Love, there is a wide diffusion of love towards the world. *Bonum diffusivum sui,* said Saint Thomas Aquinas: a love which gives itself, diffuses itself, everywhere, unselfishly and with utter care for the whole creation. The doctrine of the divine Triunity is saying this, with its insistence that what is seen of God's working in the world gives us a glimpse of what God must be in himself. We are persons precisely because we are also social creatures; God is like persons, because in him too there is both personality and sociality.

God the Father is the basic cosmic thrust whose "nature

and name is Love." God the Son is the movement of that Love outward in self-expression—and I venture even to capitalize this and write Self-Expression since in God that outgoing is so much himself that it must be divine, "very God of very God." John's Gospel says that "the Word," God in Self-Expression, was "in the beginning," as a matter of enduring principle, "with God" and "was God." As a man's activity, a woman's caring, are not something added to that person but truly *are* that person, so God's Self-Expression is himself as he gives and gives and gives, without ceasing and without diminishment. Of that Self-Expression, so far as human existence is in the picture, the supreme human expression is in the Man Jesus: this is the significance of the incarnation of God in Christ.

Yet we cannot rest content at that point. We need to go on to say that God the Holy Spirit is the mode of divine life in which God himself makes possible, through inspiration, in-forming, disclosing, and enabling, the right response to his outgoing Love. Here once more we should capitalize: we are talking about Response, so real, so full, so inclusive, and so all-compelling (albeit by persuasion, lure, and invitation, rather than by the compulsion exercised by coercive force), that we dare to affirm that here we find, and are found by, God himself. The Father is God: the eternal Son or Word or Self-Expression is God: the Holy Spirit or Response is God; and yet there are not three Gods but one God, who is blessed forever.

In those last words I have been paraphrasing a very old Christian doctrinal formulation called the *Quicunque Vult,* sometimes known as the Athanasian Creed (this latter is a false attribution, since the early theologian Athanasius had nothing to do with it; it comes as we now know from post-Augustinian times). Of all the traditional formulations this often seems one of the most arid and academic. Nevertheless it does contain occasional gems of Christian insight, not least when it asserts: "This is the

Catholic Faith, that we worship Godhead in Trinity and Trinity in Unity." The doctrine of the Triunity of God is not a matter of speculation; it is a matter of Christian adoration and praise and for that very reason a matter of concrete practical Christian living. Or as one of the canticles in the Prayer Book phrases it:

> Let us bless the Father and the Son with the Holy Spirit:
> Let us praise and exalt *him* forever.

VI

Church and Sacraments

In many quarters today the Church is receiving "a bad press." Critics accuse it of unwarranted conservatism, saying that it has utterly failed to "keep up with the times." They speak of its stuffiness, its dullness, its worship as boring and its leadership as unimaginative. Even those who accept the Christian faith sometimes wonder if participation in the institutional and organized religious community is not more of a hindrance than a help to them in their discipleship. Indeed there are not lacking those who say that the Church is dying, if not already dead; in the latter case, what appear to be signs of life are only the galvanic twitchings of a corpse.

Further, many who themselves belong to the Church and are active in its affairs wonder whether there is any *theological* significance in its existence. Of course it is there as a matter of sociological fact, like service clubs, Chambers of Commerce, and the like. But can the Church be considered an essential part of the total Christian enterprise? Is it so essential that when we are working out a theology—by which, let us recall, we are not talking about something purely speculative or theoretical and only for the experts but about a coherent and consistent statement of Christian faith and life implicit in the existence of any and every Christian—that when we are thus "doing theology," we simply cannot avoid including

the Christian community as a constituent part of the total
enterprise we know as Christianity?

It is with this question, and with the corollaries which
will necessarily follow once we concede the inescapable
importance of the Christian community, that we shall
concern ourselves in this chapter. I must begin by saying
very plainly that to my mind the Christian community *is*
an essential part of the Christian enterprise, even going
so far as to insist that without participation in its life nobody can properly be called a Christian in any complete
sense of that word. I say this, knowing very well the
inadequacies, defects, failures, dullness, drabness, sometimes the sheer stupidity, of much in the Church as we
know it. As one who has been more or less intimately
involved in many of the "official Church's" affairs, I am
perhaps even more conscious of this than are those who
have had a peripheral involvement, or maybe none at all,
in such matters. I too have had moments of near despair
about the Church as I see it and know it, both in its
parishes and in its top administrative agencies. Certainly
I would agree that the Church is in need of radical changing in many of its modes of activity, although I would have
to add that this conviction is itself an outgrowth of my
sense of Church-belonging and a consequence of that
truth of which the battle cry of the Reformation in the
16th century is an expression: *ecclesia reformata et
semper reformanda* ("the Church reformed and always to
be reformed"). I say this, too, with my own allegiance to
what I may describe as the "Catholic" view of the nature
and purpose of the Church; and I take heart from the fact
that precisely in circles where that view is held we see the
most devoted and concerned effort at such reformation.
Vatican II has made this clear enough, so far as Roman
Catholicism is concerned; and in the Anglican Communion there is an equal awareness of this, perhaps more

particularly among those of us who used to be styled "An-
glo-Catholics."

William Temple once wrote that when Jesus withdrew
his visible presence from men he left behind him, not a
teaching or a theology or a set of ideas, but a community
or fellowship. What happened as a matter of plain history
was the emergence of a group of men and women who in
their response to the reality of Jesus Christ found themselves knit together, so much knit together that they
formed a fellowship with specific convictions, with a specific way of worshiping God, and with a specific task given
them. They constituted a distinct and identifiable society
in the world of their time. And for them, to be a Christian
was to belong to that society, however much others outside the society might share some of their beliefs and
accept some of their convictions about moral behavior.
Anybody who reads the letters of Paul and John can see
this clearly.

The mention of Paul and John brings to mind their
language about the Church. The former uses several
analogies but the one most frequent in his writing is "the
Body of Christ." Christ is the head, those who are Christians are the members, and the two together constitute a
totality in which, as with our own bodies, the mind or soul
expresses itself through the members. John does not use
this image but he speaks of the "vine and the branches."
The vine stands for Christ and the branches for those who
belong to him as his disciples; without the vine there
would be no vitality in the branches, since they depend
upon and are part of the vine although not identical with
it in any simple sense. Of course both of these images can
be pushed to absurd extremes; but if they are seen *as*
images or symbolic descriptions, they can help us greatly
in our recognizing the essential relationship between the
Lord and his people, a relationship which is so intimate

that one without the other is less than the full truth.

Nor is it difficult to understand how community is important in religious matters, since (as we have already urged when speaking about God and again about human nature) human beings are social beings. Personality and sociality are two sides of one coin. Nobody can be genuinely human unless he or she is also in relationship with others of the race. If this is the case with ordinary existence, so to say, it is even more true when we are responding to the lure and attraction of God—the cosmic drive requires that we shall answer back, not only as this and that particular person but also in our "togetherness" (if one may use that now slightly worn cliché) as humans. Men and women quite naturally come together about matters that seem to them of great importance; there is nothing more important than their responding to the loving action of God toward them and for them.

If the basic structures which express the dynamic reality that is our world are not our own devising but somehow are "given" in the very nature of things, then it is possible to speak of the social pattern of human existence as the divine intention. So also, when it comes to the community of faith, we may say—and Christians have in fact always been prepared to insist—that the Christian Church is both a natural and normal human grouping and also a divinely purposed, divinely created, community. This should not suggest that the ecclesiastical institution is not open to study by the usual methods employed in sociological investigation; to talk in that fashion would be to deny the genuine human quality of the Church. But it *is* to say that the Church is not exhaustively described when we have employed those methods; "there's more to it than that," since the Church is the place where, the series of happenings through which, God in Christ does reach out to and sustain his children in a specially intensive and caring manner.

But did Jesus found the Church, as somebody might found or establish some club or society today? The answer here must be no. It has been said that Jesus did not found the Church but that the Church is *founded on him:* "The Church's one foundation is Jesus Christ her Lord." In and through the total event of Christ there came into existence in the world this particular community which builds itself upon him and his action; it sees him, not as its founder, but as its head and Lord. And that is much more significant than if we looked at the Church as if it were concerned simply to propagate certain ideas and urge certain ethical and religious standards. The Church exists so that Christ may be present still, in the here-and-now of our living. Through its ministrations and worship, through its discipleship manifested in those who are its members, indeed through the totality which constitutes what the Prayer Book calls "the mystical Body of Christ," the historic person and work of Christ are brought out of the past into the present, so that what might very well have been a life lost in the mists of ancient history becomes a vital and inescapable fact in the contemporary world.

In doing and being this, the Church is *one.* Of course at the present time there are what we style denominational divisions, but in its inner reality there is a basic unity which consists in the working of Christ, or of God through Christ, in the world. Further, to continue with what traditionally have been known as the "notes of the Church," the Christian fellowship is *holy.* We need to understand that the primary significance of that word is not moral perfection, although the striving after such moral goodness is the consequence of the Church's "holiness." The word "holy" means here primarily that the Church is God's Church, since it is the Body of Christ; it is not a human invention and hence it must both understand its divine mission and give its final loyalty to that which God wants done in the world. The Church also is *catholic,* a word which includes the idea of universality, its being for all men and women in all times and places, but which has its deepest sense in wholeness or an "organic" quality of life. This is a consequence of the insistence on the Church as Christ's Body, of course. A body is not an organization but an organism in which each part affects and influences every other part. So too the Church's faith, worship, and life are knit together in an interpenetrating fashion; so too the Lord of the Church and those who belong to him in the Church are knit together to such a degree that it can be said that "we dwell in him and he in us." Finally, remembering the last of the notes of the Church, it is *apostolic.* That word comes from a Greek verb and might be translated as "sentness." The Church is in the world with a job to do, not of its own imagining but of divine purposing. In carrying out its job or mission, the Church is apostolic in still another sense: it is in continuity with the past, "built upon the prophets and apostles," so that it may be identified for what it is by the way in which it continues in the world the faith taught by, the worship engaged in, and the life manifested through, the earliest of its members, the very "apostles" themselves.

The Christian fellowship is also marked by a ministering function. It has a job to do, as we have said; "every member of the same," says the Good Friday collect, has "his vocation and ministry." That tells us that each Christian is a minister, a servant (for that is what the word "minister" really means) of Christ to the world. As it happens, however, some members of the Church who have been ordained have a particular function within the life of the whole organism. That function is to proclaim the gospel—the good news of God's action in Christ; to celebrate the sacraments—the normal mode of Christian worship, to which we shall turn in a moment; and to "shepherd the flock"—to care for men and women so that they may know the divine love, experience the divine compassion, act for the divine righteousness, and be built up in Christian life. Those three—proclaiming, celebrating, and caring—are the special duty of the persons whom we call "ordained ministers." They have no status or position which sets them entirely apart from others in the Church; it is their function which counts, since they are "ministering agents" for the mission and obligation of the Church as a whole. It has been one of the glories of the Anglican tradition that it has stressed this representative and ministering interpretation of the ordained person. In some other circles, the tendency has been either to separate the clergy from the people or to identify the clergy with the people. In the first instance, the result has been to set up a great gulf between the "teaching Church" and the "learning Church," as the two have been called. In the second instance, there is nothing distinctive about the ordained person's responsibility, beyond having been chosen as a layperson who does this or that at the convenience of the congregation. But the ordained person *does* do specific things, as a glance at any Christian denomination, even those which disclaim any speciality of function, will demonstrate. Why not, then, see that there are indeed "diversities of gifts" within the Church, while at the same time there is "one Spirit" which animates and works in the total community? This does not separate the ordained from the unordained; all it does is to say that nobody can readily and appropriately do everything and that some distinction in function, provided it is always function for the whole, is valuable and essential to the healthy life of the Body.

So much for the theological interpretation of the Church—its social reality is entirely natural, it shares in the dynamic quality of all existence, it is in relationship to the life of the world and not over-against or apart from the world. In other words, as the community of those who are growing in love as they are conformed to the image of God in Christ, the Church's existence is in accordance with the pattern which we have seen running through everything in creation. The Church remembers its past, it decides and acts in the present, and it aims at the future, when God's Kingdom will come, in his good pleasure, "on earth as it is in heaven."

We have said that the normal mode of Christian worship is sacramental; we might also have said that the whole Christian life is sacramental. For what is a sacrament? It is the working of a divine or more than human reality in and through a created, finite, and hence limited instrument. A kiss is the "sacramental" occasion when the invisible love of one person is conveyed through a physical act to which the other responds. So the world is a material and physical creation in and through which God works his will and accomplishes his purpose, like the mind which uses the body to express itself.

Another way of putting this is to speak of the world as an incarnational world. In Jesus Christ, says Christian faith, God has "incarnated"—embodied and "enmanned" himself—in a genuine human existence. This does not mean, however, that only there has God been acting incarnationally. Rather, he is constantly incarnating himself in his world, identifying himself with it, acting through it, making his presence in it known and felt through the happenings which take place in it. Of that everlasting movement of God to and in his world the event of Jesus Christ is the supreme and decisive instance, so far as humans are concerned.

The sacramental rites of the Christian community are in accordance with this basic truth about things. In them material or physical things, creaturely and finite events or happenings, are used by God as the instrumental channels through which he makes himself available to us and by which we may make our faithful response to him.

Whether or not all of the Church's sacramental rites were explicitly "instituted" by Christ himself or came into existence through the deepening insight of the Church as the Holy Spirit "took of the things of Christ and declared them unto us," the truth remains that in all of them a way is provided for human worship of and for intimate contact with God as manifested in Jesus Christ. Thus it is entirely natural and completely understandable that the normal and usual modes of Christian observance are sacramental rites which have come down to us from our Christian past.

In this chapter we have space to comment upon only two of these sacramental rites: Baptism and the Eucharist or Holy Communion. The others, to greater or less degree recognized under some guise by all Christians, belong in the same general category—the gift of the Holy Spirit when children and others are brought to be "confirmed"; the words spoken by an ordained minister when he assures a penitent person or a congregation that God does forgive, and has forgiven, the offenses against the divine Love to which they have confessed; the blessing which the Church gives to those who are being married, so that their union of bodies may be a true union of persons; the ordaining of persons who are to function for the Church in its proclamation, celebration, and shepherding ministry to the world; and the prayers for, with the possible anointing of, sick persons so that they may face suffering and even death with equanimity and in Christian faith. It would seem that in one way or another almost all the exigencies of life are provided for through this range of sacramental acts, each of them involving some physical thing or some physical gesture, and each of them conveying God's care and concern.

Baptism is the rite of initiation into the Christian community. Through the use of water, poured on the candidate, and with the invocation of the Spirit, reception into the fellowship is effected. There are two aspects of Baptism, each of them equally important. One is the entrance through that act into the new life of the Christian community; the other is the enabling of the new member to begin life as "a faithful soldier and servant of Christ," with the prayer that he may continue in this loyalty "unto his life's end." The entrance into the Church is indeed an entering upon something new. By natural birth each of us is a member of the human race, potentially a lover who will make actual the capacity to live in love with neighbor and with God. But "that which by nature he cannot have" is membership in the Body of Christ. Each of us must be brought into that Body and made a member incorporate in it. This is one part of Baptism.

The other part is the enabling of the new Christian to continue faithfully the baptismal profession. Traditionally this has been stated in a negative, not a positive fashion —which has been unfortunate. It has been talked about in terms of "the washing away of sin," as if an accumulation of dirt needed to be removed before the candidate could be accepted by God. Put positively, what is signified here is the opening of new possibilities of life with God in love, of which "sin" is a denial and contradiction. Perhaps we might say that it is rather like the potential transformation which occurs when a child is taken from the hard and harsh life of a city into the open and gracious life of the countryside, with healthy air and sunshine to help him grow into the man he should become.

Baptism, therefore, establishes initial participation in the Christian community through a sacramental rite in which words spoken and water poured symbolize and signify, and therefore effect, a translation into the splendid existence made available to us by God in Jesus Christ. The Eucharist or Holy Communion is the means whereby this existence is nourished, strengthened, enriched, and continued through the whole course of the believer's life. The Eucharist has its origin in the last meal which Jesus had with his friends, when "on the night in which he was betrayed" he took the bread and wine of the common meal and did with them something that the early Christians were convinced he meant them to continue. He broke and blessed bread, making it the sign of his own self-giving; he shared the cup of wine, making it the sign of his sharing with them and they with him in the Kingdom of God. They were to do this "in remembrance of him."

Note that they *did* this: the Eucharist is something done, not a matter of words said or thoughts entertained. Note also that "in remembrance of him" must be understood in the *Jewish* meaning of "remembrance." It is not simply thinking back to the past and wishing "we might have been with him then." For the Jews "to make memorial" had a very different significance; for them it was God's bringing a past event into the immediacy of present experience, turning "the dead past" into a living past known in the present moment. When the traditional Jew observes the Seder feast of the Passover, remembering God's deliverance of his people at the Red Sea, he would not for a second think of this as mere historical reminiscence. On the contrary, he believes that in his observing that feast, God here-and-now, at this very moment, is delivering his people and making himself known to them.

The Eucharist is "remembrance" of Christ in *that* sense. It is also Jesus' taking to himself those who gather at the Holy Table, uniting them with himself in his self-offering to the Father. And as such, it is a sacrificial action, although the priest is Christ himself, just as he is also the one who is offered—the victim. The Eucharist, furthermore, is the presentness of Christ himself to the faith of those who come to receive the blessed bread and wine. This is a better word than the older phrase "Christ's presence," since that might suggest a spatial presence of the Lord; what is here intended is a genuine making-present in a contemporary action of an action accomplished in the past through the whole existence of Jesus in "the days of his flesh" when he was with men on earth in a visible fashion. Finally, the Eucharist is the establishment of a communion between God and his children, made real in Christ himself. As Christ shared our humanity, so we are united with our human brethren (and especially our Christian brethren) *in him;* and as Christ was also the decisive activity of God in human terms, we are united with God our Father *in him.*

All of this is through bread and wine, material things that belong to our common life. This is sacrament *par excellence:* and that is why it is characteristic of Christians to worship God through the things of the world, the world in which he is always at work and from which he will never separate himself because he loves it and us and wants to make it and us his very own.

VII
Fulfillment and Destiny

For a great many of us the chief reason for believing the Christian faith is that it seems to promise survival after death, both for ourselves and for those whom we love. Indeed it might be said that there are those whose primary concern is with this survival and whose trust in God is a function of that concern. I must confess that such an attitude appears to me to be utterly wrong. It is altogether too much like investing one's funds in a guaranteed trust, where the main interest is in the interest we may receive. A verse in a Victorian hymn unconsciously states just this:

> Whatever, Lord, we give to thee
> A thousand-fold repaid will be;
> Then gladly will we give to thee
> Who givest all.

I can only regard that sort of religion as specious.

As a matter of fact, in Jewish history belief in significant personal survival after death came fairly late in the life of the community. There had been acceptance of a shadowy half-existence after death for the pale ghost of the soul; this was called "sheol" and in the Psalms is usually translated "hell." The Jew believed that he was "made of the dust of the earth" upon which God had "breathed" so that a "living creature" came into existence. Since God's "breath," somehow communicated to human beings and enjoying thereafter a kind of existence of its own, could never be utterly extinguished, the Jew was prepared to accept that *that* went on, after death; but the vivid and warm reality which we mean by personal life did not continue. Only during the period of the Maccabean Wars, when Jewish patriots were martyred for their faith, did the typical Jew begin to claim that God would never let such courageous people undergo complete extinction; instead, they would "be raised from the dead" in some fashion so that they might share in the restoration of Israel which Judaism confidently expected.

This belief in resurrection from the dead, as we ought to phrase it, was refined and developed in a more "spiritual" direction—with less stress on actual physical or bodily elements—in later Judaism and it was this which Paul, along with most Jews of his time, believed to be the destiny of men.

The Christian thinkers of the first centuries added to this ideas which were common in the Graeco-Roman world of the time, ideas having to do with "the immortality of the soul." Unlike the Jews, who believed that man was a body-soul unity, the Greeks tended to think of man as essentially a soul introduced into and resident in a body —a very different idea. Furthermore, they thought that the soul could be, and at death was, separated from the body. Hence the soul might continue as an indestructible entity when the body died and decayed. The marriage of Jewish belief in resurrection and Greek belief in immortality was never a very happy one, largely because it introduced into Christian thinking a whole series of insuperable problems about human nature, the place of the material world, the sort of "life after death" which ought to be envisaged, and the like. None the less, this strange combination of incompatibles has continued and by many it is still thought to be *the* Christian "hope," although in recent years New Testament scholars, building also on

Old Testament material, have tried to dissociate the two and work out some supposedly biblical view which will put main emphasis on "resurrection" and assign to "immortality of the soul" a very secondary place.

So much for a brief historical sketch. What then can we today, in our attempt to work out a theology for lay people, confidently affirm about this hope for human life? What will follow is my own tentative suggestion, building upon the two things which in all that has been said have been our chief resources. Those two things, we recall, are the enduring Christian witness of faith founded upon the action of God in Jesus Christ *and* the knowledge we now possess about the world and human existence in that world.

In the first place, let me quote some fine words of the great French Jesuit palaeontologist Pierre Teilhard de Chardin. In one of his books (found in the collection *Oeuvres,* Paris 1969, Vol. 10, pp. 135–136), Teilhard wrote: "The problem of personal survival *per se* doesn't worry me much. Once the fruit of my life is received up into One who is eternal, what can it matter whether I am egotistically conscious of it or have joy of it? I am quite sincere when I say that my personal felicity does not interest me. To be happy it is enough to know that the best of me passes on forever into One who is more beautiful and greater than I."

I suppose that these words will be like a dash of cold water for many who read or hear them. And yet, coming as they do from a man who was profoundly Christian in attitude and outlook and who, as comments made in his last days showed, believed in some persistence of identity after death, do they not make very plain that the basic Christian stress is upon God and not upon our own personal survival? I have said that Christianity is a theocentric faith, focused upon God; Teilhard's words are a further expression of just that theocentrism. He was saying that it is less than fully Christian to center one's thoughts on one's own supposed survival, while it is exactly the Christian emphasis on God that has made it possible to affirm that the fruit of one's life will be "received up into One" who himself is everlasting and is much more "beautiful" than human existence can be. What is more, he was concerned to say that what he styled (perhaps too extremely) the "egotistical" demand that one must be "conscious" of that reception, is not in and of itself necessary to the Christian conviction that God loves, cares for, and is implicated in each and every human life.

In speaking in this way, Teilhard touched upon the difficulty with the conventional view: namely, that it may be a "dog-in-the-manger" attitude, refusing to recognize God's proper place, saying that one will not cooperate in the working out of God's will unless one is certain of one's own reward for doing so. Nobody, certainly no Christian, can rightly make any such *claims upon God.* On the contrary, all is to be *ad majorem dei gloriam,* "to God's greater glory"; and the wonderful thing is that God's glory is not divine self-aggrandizement but rather the increasing full expression of "pure unbounded Love" in every time and place.

Then what about our hope of survival? I wish to say that not *all* the interest in survival is the kind of self-centered business to which I have just referred. A good deal of it is the urgent feeling that those whom "we have loved long since and lost awhile" cannot, must not, be cast away as if they were rubbish. For after all, to love is to experience something of eternality. Love has about it a quality of everlastingness which not even "the last enemy" death can utterly destroy. The rightness of this feeling can be preserved, however, without falling victim to Teilhard's sharp criticism and without taking literally the popular mythology of "life after death," which so often speaks of it as if it were just a continuation, without fundamental

change, of what we know and enjoy in this present existence. The way to get at this, with a theology adequate to
our contemporary Christian stance, is by grasping the real
significance of Paul's teaching that "we are risen with
Christ" and that it is in *his* resurrection that his human
brethren are to share. We turn, therefore, to that Pauline
teaching.

Paul puts the resurrection of Christ in the central place.
There are texts in which resurrection is given a meaning
that applies to believers or to all men, but the main thrust
of the material is toward asserting that it is *Christ* who is
risen; and what is said about the resurrection of others
follows from this firm conviction that to be "in Christ" (a
phrase which Paul uses more than a hundred times in one
context or another) *is* "to be risen with him." Nowhere
does this come through so clearly, perhaps, as in the
Apostle's teaching about Baptism, where we are told that
by "putting on Christ" the person baptized is incorporated into him and shares with him not only life in this
world but also life "in heavenly places." Nothing is said
about any natural "immortality," since Paul and the primitive Christian community thought more naturally in
terms of the Jewish conception of resurrection. Human
destiny, then, was found in the incorporation of men and
women into Christ, into his risen life where he had been
taken by God and which was to be shared with those who
were his members.

What did these early Christian believers intend to say
when they spoke in this fashion of the Christ into whose
risen life the faithful were incorporated and in which they
themselves were convinced they were already participant? Certainly attention was centered on Jesus in his
historical human existence and in what had happened in
him, to him, and around him. But they had also come to
believe that in the complex event which we call Jesus
Christ there was the embodiment of God's continued

working in the affairs of history. As we have already noted earlier, this was why they could speak of Jesus as the very "en-manning" of the eternal Word.

Thus, to say that Christ is risen from the dead is not to say only that Jesus, that Man in that time and place, is risen. It is to say that the activity of God in his Self-Expression, and supremely in the one in whom that Self-Expression was dominant, has found its focus in Jesus. It is to say that this activity of God includes forever Jesus and all that he has effected. More particularly, it is to say that those who are members of Christ, who have responded to his grasping of them and have known themselves incorporated into his Body, are so much a part of him that in his risen life they are with him. What has happened in and to him, in his concrete specificity as Jesus and in his embodiment of the divine activity to which the faithful respond, happens also and applies also to all who have been united with him in faith and discipleship. To be "in Christ," therefore, is to be in him as risen from the dead. Nor is such participation for a short time only; it is an abiding reality. Now and always, once the relationship has occurred, it does and will continue.

In our next and last chapter we shall have something to say about the millions of men and women who have not known Jesus Christ in the specific historical sense. For the present, let us recognize that this Pauline and general early Christian picture will help us to get our own ideas straight. *I* am not in the center. *Christ* is in the center and he *is* the center; and he is this because in him God has acted decisively and with speciality. What I am and what I am to become if I am faithful and loyal, my destiny and my hope, are always in him. And *he is risen*. God has received him, having "raised him from death"; and in receiving him God has received "all that appertains to the perfection" of human nature, to use a phrase from one of the Thirty-Nine Articles of the Church of England. The notion of resurrection is, therefore, a way of saying that all materiality, all history, all relationships known and experienced by human beings, have found their focus in this supreme instance of humanity. If every person is in some small degree such a focus of matter, history, and relationships, Christ (meaning Jesus and all that happened to him, in him, around him, and through him) is preeminently such a focus—and to speak of his "body" is to indicate everything which constituted his existence as a Man. All of that has been received by God into the divine life; it has become forever part of what some of us call "God's consequent or actual nature," which is to say, God in the concrete sense of the One who is ceaselessly identified with and related to all creation.

In the Old Testament, we have seen, the meaning of the word "remember" is profound. Its significance is not historical recollection but a genuine "making alive" of that which has happened in the past, at this or that particular moment of time. The memory which is here in view is livingness, not the "dead past." We can speak confidently of the *divine* memory. By speaking of it we are pointing to God's bringing all the past into the immediacy of present awareness—nothing is lost from that immediacy, save that which is so alien to the divine nature of love that it can find no place in God's inner life. The creative movement of the world, with its every detail, its every point of "importance" great or small, its every contribution to the purpose of God in furthering love in the world, is experienced in God, including the anguish as well as the joy, the suffering as well as the triumph.

To think of God's memory as if it were simply showing over and over again some film of past events would be to misunderstand completely what we are saying. Canon David Edwards of Westminster Abbey has said this about divine memory: "Certainly one great advantage of thinking about God's memory of us is that it helps us to see that our eternal life is more than this life going on forever; it is a share in God's life and God's glory, when nothing is between God and us. Does that involve what is commonly called 'personal survival'? Well, not if that phrase means that no big difference is made by death. . . . [But] God will continue to love *you*, the *you* he knows, and *you* will have your own place in the glory of God" (*Asking Them Questions*, Oxford 1973, p. 56).

In this profound sense *Jesus* is remembered by God; and as a corollary of that remembrance, we who are one with Christ are also remembered by him, as Canon Edwards has insisted. This is the basic Christian theological affirmation and it makes all questions of "conscious" awareness of the fact quite secondary, even though they are still important. Surely it is legitimate for us to hope that this may be the case; and after all the Church has traditionally spoken in just that way: the *hope* of everlasting life. But however we may wish to see this point, the central assertion of faith stands firm—it is our being incorporated into the life of Christ and hence also into the divine remembrance of Christ.

I have been engaging in what quite obviously is a sort of demythologizing, to use the language of the contemporary German Christian thinker Rudolf Bultmann. What I have been attempting is to get at the fundamental affirmation which is behind and in all the symbolical, mythological, and pictorial language we necessarily use when we try to talk of matters which are far and away beyond our experience in this present existence. But in doing this I have sought to be entirely faithful to the abiding significance of what is being said in those images or pictures; and I have wanted to get at the existential import of this for us today—what this means for you and me in our present-day life on this planet. Or we could say that our concern has been with finding what the pictorial material can signify for us in concrete experience. Let me now try to sum this up.

First of all, any man or woman who has genuinely responded to "the love of God which was in Christ Jesus" has been united with that divine Love. This divine Love, embodied in Jesus, was of such intensity that not even death could defeat it; indeed, nothing can defeat the love of God in any final sense. It is the only truly strong thing in the world. Thornton Wilder wrote in *The Bridge of San Luis Rey* that "love is the only survival, the only meaning"; and he was speaking precisely of the Love which is God.

To know oneself caught up into that Love, to share in it, to be used by it, *is* "eternal life," in John's phrase. It *is* "resurrection from among the dead." To seek to exist apart from that Love is death. Here is the awful possibility which we must face, even if we are at the same time confident that the Love is so great that it will "never let us go" but will strive always to win us to itself. Anybody who has begun to "live in love" has also begun to "live in Love." Anyone who has thus begun such a life is already united with the existence of Jesus Christ, whether Jesus himself has been known or even heard of: for God's love, and Love as God, is focused in, although it is not confined to, the specific historical existence of the Man Jesus. To be thus in the Love that is God, or in the Lover who is God, is to be in God's "consequent nature," in the divine reality as that reality has been affected by what has gone on and goes on and will go on in the created and finite world which is ours and in the historical existence which we know as our own. This is why the feeling that to love is to have some sense of everlastingness is so right and sound and proper. The testimony of quite ordinary people that they have this profound feeling is no delusion; it touches the very heart of reality and is in accordance with how things actually do go in the world.

I trust that what has been said so far will not seem abstract and lacking in vividness. I have tried to be as clear as I could about a subject which is very complex. And I conclude now by saying something more about what is here involved, with reference to the topics that commonly are styled the "four last things" and which often are the theme of sermons during the Advent season: death, judgment, heaven, and hell.

First, you and I are going to die. This is the one absolute certainty, the finality of our mortal existence. Nowadays death is an obscene topic which we avoid or cover up; the painting of a corpse to make it seem lifelike is but one example of our sense of repulsion in the presence of the fact of death. But there is another sense in which we all die. Every day each of us is dying to our past—not entirely, of course, since what has happened in that past has its causal efficacy in the present and to a large degree we are what our past still makes us. Yet the past is "over and done with" in at least one sense; and we are given the opportunity to do what Tennyson notes in one of his bits of verse: "rise on stepping-stones of our dead selves/to higher things." We can accept the death of our past; we can die to our habits of selfishness and pride; we can move on toward the future, helped by the gracious influences which seek to affect us and which in the last resort are God's working through the things of this world.

Then there is the fact of judgment. Maybe a better word here would be "appraisal." Every day we are being appraised in respect to the degree to which we have sought rightly to respond to the lure of the good, true, just, beautiful, responsible, and loving. In this respect we can evaluate our contribution; and others are always doing the same, some kindly and some unkindly. But there is also an appraisal of our whole span of existence at the moment when we come to die. Face to face with such a finality, we may well ask how much or how little we have moved in the direction of becoming, as we are intended to become, created and finite lovers, with many defects and failures yet with enormous possibilities as well. What has this life of ours *really* amounted to? How would we ourselves appraise it? How would others do so? Finally there is the "grand appraisal," symbolized in Christian terms by talk of "the last judgment"; and that has to do with whether the whole cosmic enterprise, including our own small part in it, has been worthwhile, has accomplished anything, has been in some degree a way of furthering God's purpose of more love at more times and in more places. Hence appraisal or judgment is a continuing and an inescapable reality.

What about heaven and hell? We need not await a future apart from this life to be blessed or damned. Here in this present moment we can be in heaven or we can be in hell. Heaven is the joy known when we are functioning rightly as human persons, doing the true, good, honest, just, and loving things, and finding our existence moving towards genuine integration in that which will fulfil and complete us and which even now we know by anticipation in small samples. Hell is the sense of disintegration, of falling apart, of failure and rejection, on those occasions when we know that we have refused to become what was in us to become and have preferred to center everything on our own ideas, likings, ambitions, and desires, to the exclusion of others and in contempt of the God who lovingly entices us to him.

Thus the "four last things" are matters of present experience for anybody who has the insight and the capacity to look honestly into him or herself and face the facts, good or bad, which that look discloses.

The way in which and the manner by which Love will ultimately accomplish its work in us, should we be moving toward our proper goal, are not known to us here and now. Most of the pictures of heaven (or of hell) have been childish, we may think; for us today they are usually incredible. At the same time they have witnessed to the conviction that God never "lets down" his creation nor his human children. We can say boldly that the departed are safe and satisfied in God's love. Christians can go on to say with utter confidence that any who have been united with the cosmic Lover, however slight their response to him has been, are caught up into God's life, where beyond death Love abides. That ought to be sufficient for us. The Love disclosed in Jesus Christ is the truth about everything and can be trusted in any and every circumstance, even in death itself.

VIII
Living the Faith Today

Throughout this book, I have written as a defender and exponent of the kind of Christian thinking known as "Process theology," based especially, as we have said, upon the work of the philosopher Alfred North Whitehead. Whitehead developed an interpretation of the world which stressed its dynamic, energetic, societal character and laid great emphasis on the primacy of what he called "persuasion" (or love in action) in the affairs of that world. I take this Process position, not for speculative reasons although these are important enough, but because I believe this theology is most suited for a coherent and consistent statement of the Christian faith for our own day and time. I believe that it provides a vehicle for our re-conception of that faith, which will enable us to recover important and often forgotten aspects of it, because I think it is congruous with the total biblical way of seeing things, and because I am sure that it offers a vehicle which will help to make the faith "available," as the saying goes, for our own age.

I shall now try to develop further some of the insights present in this kind of theology and also to see how they help us to face and answer certain difficulties to faith which many people feel nowadays. I do not intend to suggest a sort of guide to concrete problems of daily life nor a manual for Christian discipleship. This is a task for others. I happen to be a theologian, for good or ill; and I had better stick to my vocation.

In one of Whitehead's books there is a fine paragraph which I now quote in part: "The essence of Christianity is the appeal to the life of Christ as a revelation of the nature of God and of his agency in the world. The record is fragmentary, inconsistent, and uncertain . . . but there can be no doubt as to what elements in the record have evoked a response from all that is best in human nature. The Mother, the Child, and the bare manger: the lowly man, homeless and self-forgetful, with his message of peace, love, and sympathy; the suffering, the agony, the tender words as life ebbed, the final despair: and the whole with the authority of supreme victory" (*Adventures of Ideas,* Cambridge, 1933, p. 170).

I add to that quotation two others from the same thinker. The first of these immediately follows the words I have cited: "The power of Christianity lies in its revelation in act of that which Plato [and I should insert here, "and others too"] divined in theory." The second, from one of Whitehead's other books, is this: "The task of theology is to show how the world is founded on something beyond transient fact, and how it issues in something beyond the perishing of occasions."

These quotations are given here because they get at the heart of man's basic problem: what is the world really like? Phrased somewhat differently, how do things really *go?* Or, put in the usual idiom of the theologian, what is God like and what does God do? People may not always be vividly conscious of this kind of question, yet it *is* the one to which they seek an answer in all that they say and do and think. The reason for this is simply that human existence can only have any abiding significance if it is founded, as Whitehead saw, on that which is "beyond transient fact," beyond the day-by-day matters we all know so well. The human heart and mind desires a significance that will be "beyond the perishing of occasions," beyond the inevitable ending of our mortal existence, and beyond the extinction of the planet upon which our existence occurs.

There is a story, which I have often had occasion to tell, about a little girl who was found one Sunday afternoon busily engaged in making a drawing. Her mother, a puritanical kind of person, said to the child, "You mustn't draw things on Sunday." To which the girl replied, "Oh, what I'm drawing is all right to do on a Sunday." To this the mother answered, "Well, what *are* you drawing?" "A picture of God," said the child. And then the mother said, "You can't do that. Nobody knows what God looks like." The child's response was very direct: "They *will*, when I get done."

Now that story, silly as it is, makes a point. The answer to the big question I have posed above is plainly that in one sense nobody knows. Nobody can work out with certainty a sketch of how the world really goes—of what God really is and what God really does. Yet the whole history of human religion is the record of human attempts to do just this. Men and women have done it on the basis of intimations and hints, of bits of human experience and human observation; and they have "divined in theory" that in and through everything there is what I have called a deep thrust or drive, essentially persuasive in character, which is both supremely important and supremely creative and which is also worshipful as the source of human "refreshment and comradeship"—once again to use some words of Whitehead about the function of religion in human experience.

We have seen, however, that the central assertion of the specifically Christian faith is God's priority to human thinking. That assertion is a bold declaration about *God's having drawn his own picture,* and having drawn it in a human life which human beings can therefore understand and apprehend since it comes to them in their own familiar terms. In other words, Christianity talks about the life of Christ as a "revelation of the nature of God and of his agency in the world." It *comes to us;* it is not a matter of our human devising or our human speculation, but a fact of history, to which men and women may respond and from which they may work out a way of seeing things—themselves, the world, and God—which makes sense of, and which gives sense to, the whole range of experience. Of course a rational statement of what this means must be humanly undertaken and will be as much subject to revision as any other piece of human reasoning. The originating fact, however, is *there,* in history, in a Man, in one who suffered as he also taught, who lived among us and died as we do, and who is believed to have conquered death since his life was such that "it could not be holden by" death.

The power of Christian faith lies in its being not merely an idea, important as that might be; nor a speculation, illuminating as that might be; nor a moral ideal, useful as that might be. Its power is found in our being given "in act," through an event in human history, the "revelation of the nature of God and of the divine agency." It is this which has "evoked a response from all that is best in human nature."

In this book we have endeavoured to spell out some of the consequences which follow from this fact. Our concern has been to see that the Man of Nazareth demands a response, either negative in denying that he has anything to tell us about the nature of God, the world, and ourselves, or positive in providing a clue which by our commitment we may find indicative of the truth about God, that world, and ourselves. Underneath all the different theologies of the Christian centuries, some of them harsh in their logic and some of them very appealing; underneath the hymns and anthems, the creeds and professions, the liturgies and rites, and the moral teaching: underneath all these has been the conviction that in a supreme, focal, and decisive fashion the character of God—the quality of the basic cosmic thrust or drive—is declared in that Man, in the totality of his existence.

Anything else Christians may rightly say, therefore, is a corollary of this central conviction. The test of adequacy and Christian truth is simply the degree to which what is thought and said and done conforms or fails to conform to this criterion.

Many would like to believe the central Christian conviction but have found obstacles or stumbling-blocks to their acceptance. This is why I think it important to take an honest look at three of those stumbling-blocks, which to my mind are the most difficult and which therefore must be faced and met by anybody who would wish to enter into the company of Christian believers.

The first has to do with the "miraculous." It is tied in with what seems to many a tendency to demand assent to incredible legends which so contradict all we think we know about the world that no thinking person could do other than reject them. I shall not concern myself here with the specific stories that have created this difficulty, beyond saying that long and dedicated work on the biblical material has helped in sorting out various kinds of "miracle story," some of them not very probable in themselves and others almost certainly resting upon an incident (like a healing) which may indeed have taken place.

What I should urge, however, is that we are entitled to interpret most of these tales as "miraculous" more in the telling of the story than in what may actually have occurred. Suppose that for people like the writers of the four gospels there was an urgent need to state the *real* wonder of it all: the impact that Christ himself made upon them and their sense of his utter importance for their lives. How could they tell about this save by using the patterns of thought and the explanatory symbols which were natural to them in their own age? The very fact that the tales were told shows the importance of him about whom they were told. After all, the deeply religious meaning, which is the biblical meaning, of the miraculous is not something that is unscientific and outlandish, but something that is creative of faith, expressive of profound significance, and compelling of adoring response. The stories are bearers of that faith, significance, and compulsion, however awkward may be the medium through which these are communicated to us.

A second obstacle has been the understandable tendency of much Christian preaching and teaching so to center attention on the action of *God* in Jesus that his genuine humanity has been minimized or forgotten. The result has been that Jesus sometimes seems like some *deus ex machina* intruding into the world from outside it. Whatever can we make of such an intrusion from without, lacking connection with the rest of human experience and with what God is always doing in the world? Jesus seems then to be an anomaly and nothing more. But we should not forget that throughout Christian history the Church in its official teaching has insisted on the genuine humanity of Jesus. In its early days, as we have noted in our discussion of Christ, the Church valiantly defended that humanity against those who would have made it only an "appearance" without significant reality. The Church finally defeated the "docetists," as they were called. Yet it is true, alas, that this theological victory did not entirely remove the threat of a non-human portrayal of Jesus, a threat which has been an unfortunate accompaniment of much Christian devotion as well as teaching and preaching at the popular level.

We must say that those who wish to stress Jesus' true and full humanity, with all the limitations which this involves as well as with the glory which it portrays, are entirely in line with the "official" theology of the Christian ages. Jesus is indeed one of us, in all respects sharing our human lot. But at the same time, says Christian faith, he is also the one in whom the divine activity, God in his Self-Expression, wrought its climactic and crucial deed. This God in whom Christians believe was always working through every person and through the whole of history; yet in Jesus there was something else: a fullness and adequacy which bring us to our knees in his presence rather than ask us to applaud a splendid example of human attainment. The act of God in Christ does not deny but rather completes and corrects, supplements and fulfils, all the goodness, truth, righteousness, and love which are the manifestation of God elsewhere.

Finally, some people think that to be a Christian means a rejection of everything in other religious traditions, other schemes of living, other great spiritual heroes of our race. This rejection is arrogant and supercilious, they say; and they are quite correct in saying so. But even if some Christians, including very distinguished men and women, have talked in this way, succumbing to what we might style with Arnold Toynbee "Christian imperialism," this has never been the intention of the Church's tradition. That tradition has been prepared to see Jesus as both "the desire of all nations" and the coronation of whatever is sound and true elsewhere. It has spoken of "God who at sundry times and in divers manners has spoken in times past" to men and women in many countries and cultures who have sought truth, loved justice, created loveliness, and tried to live in compassion and love.

Especially today, when we are much more keenly aware of other religious traditions like Buddhism, Hinduism, and Islam, we need to emphasize this generous attitude which has marked the great central Christian tradition. Many different devices have been sought to state this, but the fact is that these have all had as their purpose the recognition that "God has nowhere left himself without witness" among the sons and daughters of men.

How may we conceive the speciality of Christ, if we agree with that long tradition of generous recognition of truth from God given to people in other ways and of the opportunity provided for them to know him and walk with him? I believe the answer is to be found by our readiness to present the Lord of our faith as being not the supreme anomaly but the classical (that is, the focal and decisive) instance of God's working incarnationally in the world. When we speak of a "classical instance" we are not talking of "just another instance." The adjective "classical"—which means decisive and focal, as I have said—should make this clear enough. A "classical instance" provokes a response of a special sort, releases powers hitherto not experienced, and enriches and enhances our way of living so that it becomes (to use some words of the ancient Christian writer John Damascene) "a new thing." At the very same moment, however, it does not reject nor deny the *context* of that speciality in a particular event. Along these lines I suggest we can make sense for ourselves of the uniting in Christian faith of speciality *and* generality, of the particular compelling instance *and* the wider but less intensive self-disclosure of God everywhere in the world.

These three are *intellectual* obstacles. They are serious and need to be cleared away. But they are not the *real* obstacles to acceptance of Christian faith; they are not the stumbling-blocks which are *most* serious. What is the most serious obstacle? The religious word for it is "sin"; the ordinary secular word would be self-willed estrangement and arrogant determination to claim for oneself total independence. Many of us do not *want* the "grace and truth" found in Jesus, for it will come to us as judgment on our wrongdoings, wrongthinkings, and wrongspeakings. The German theologian Rudolf Bultmann has pointed out that *this* is the stumbling-block for modern men and women; and he defines it by recalling that for Paul it was human intransigeance and pride which before his conversion got in the way of his accepting Jesus as the Lord.

Perhaps there comes for most of us a time when we are wearied of our own ways, our silly fancies, our insistence on our supposed human independence. When that time comes we want a great cause which can win and keep our allegiance and command our loyalty. If and when we arrive at that point, there is always the opportunity to commit ourselves, in a great "leap of faith," to the supreme excellence, the eternal goodness, the never-failing activity of God, not in an abstract way but in the concrete, specific, and particular disclosure of God's activity in Jesus Christ. The abstract "cuts no ice," makes no demands, provides no real help for us. The concrete, specific, and particular can do this. Just as nobody can "fall in love with love," but will and can respond to love present in this or that person, so in the presentation of Jesus there is an invitation to dedicate oneself completely.

It is a risk, to be sure; but so is everything worth having and worth doing. The question which soundly based Christian thought ought to present is simply this: have you and I, and have other men and women, the courage to take that risk, to bet our lives that in Jesus we have indeed been given the "revelation of the divine nature and the divine agency" in the world? To take the risk, and to live in terms of it, is not a guarantee of security and ease of life; but it *is* to build one's existence on "something beyond the perishing of occasions."

A Study Guide for Group Use of *Unbounded Love*

Purpose of the Course:

This course is designed for men and women who want to enter into the experience of "doing theology." Using Dr. Pittenger's book as a primary resource, it seeks to enable people to reflect theologically on their own experience. The only prerequisite for the course, therefore, in addition to the commitment of time, is the willingness to look seriously at our own lives in the company of others engaged in the same task. The course seeks to take seriously the "process" way of looking at the world, in the hope that this might provide for some the opportunity to reflect on "old things in a new way."

Outline:

The course is arranged for use in a variety of settings. It can be offered in four two-hour sessions, either once a week for four weeks in the evening, or with some minimal addition in a weekend conference format. If intended as part of a Sunday morning program, each of the longer sessions can be subdivided into two one-hour sessions providing for an eight week course with an hour's session each week.

Each session is intended to draw both on our own experience and the content of the Pittenger book. Ideally, each participant should have a copy of *Unbounded Love* far enough in advance of the course to read it (and mark it) in its entirety. Individual chapters might thus be read over a second time in preparation for each session. The design of the course is as follows:

Session 1   (2 hours)—The Cosmic Thrust: Two 60 minute units based on chapters 1 ("Doing Theology Today") and 2 ("God").

Session 2   (2 hours)—The Meaning of Humanity: Two 60 minute units based on chapters 3 ("Man") and 4 ("Christ").

Session 3   (2 hours)—A Spirit-filled Community: Two 60 minute units based on chapters 5 ("The Holy Spirit") and 6 ("Church and Sacrament").

Session 4   (2 hours)—New Life in Christ: Two 60 minute units based on Chapters 7 ("Fulfillment and Destiny") and 8 ("Living the Faith Today").

MAINTAINING THE LEARNING CLIMATE:

These sessions are designed to be used by groups of between 8–12 persons. When a large number of people are involved, the purpose and introductory remarks can be presented to the total group; following this the group needs to sub-divide into smaller units. To maximize openness and trust, it is strongly urged that the same small groups be maintained throughout the entire course. At the conclusion of each session, summary reports can be made so that one group has the opportunity of giving and receiving stimuli from the others.

Since the design that follows does not suggest in detail the *how* of their implementation, the following reminder may be useful:

1. Planning and recruiting should take place far enough in advance to provide for desired participation. Generally speaking, a notice in the Sunday bulletin is not enough. At least a nucleus of people needs to be recruited on a personal basis. The *way we do* something often communicates more than *what we say*.

2. It generally helps for more than one person to be responsible for the leadership of the course. This is especially true if more than one group is involved. There should be one person in each group whose primary task is to facilitate the flow of the discussion, as well as taking responsibility for seeing that necessary supplies are readily at hand. At the conclusion of each session it helps for the leadership team to get together briefly to reflect on how things went, what changes need be made, what persons need special attention either because they talk too much or not at all.

3. During actual sessions, people need to be encouraged and assisted in speaking personally about themselves. This is crucial. Nothing deepens the life of the group more than genuine sharing of those things that provide us joy and strength, as well as those things that cause us pain and confusion.

4. Purposes for each session should be clearly stated (preferably stated on newsprint or blackboard).

5. Agendas need to be clear, who-does-what spelled out, and time frames faithfully adhered to. It helps build trust to know when the session is going to begin and when it will end.

6. Where possible, time should be allowed at the end
   of each session (or when the group bogs down) to
   deal with such questions as:

   How well are we working together?
   What changes would help deepen our exchange
   with one another?

RESOURCES:

In addition to the experience of our own lives with the
theological wisdoms provided in this book, Dr. Pittenger
also suggests the following books as useful background
reading:

Eugene H. Peters, *The Creative Advance*. St. Louis:
   Bethany Press, 1966.
Norman Pittenger, *Alfred North Whitehead*. Rich-
   mond: John Knox Press, 1969.
Norman Pittenger, *Process Thought and Christian
   Faith*. New York: MacMillan, 1968 (especially chap-
   ter 1).

A FINAL NOTE:

Be flexible! Because no two settings are the same, no
study guide can fit all situations. Tailor this guide to meet
your needs, lengthening, shortening, rewriting, or omit-
ting where necessary. Remember, the greatest resource
you have is the experience of those participating in the
course—especially when this experience is self-con-
sciously open to the movement of the Holy Spirit in your
midst.

SESSION I: The Cosmic Thrust

Purpose: To explore our experience of God in the context of "process thought."

Material Needed: Name tags, blackboard, or newsprint for each group, pencils and paper, and a copy of Appendix A for each participant.

Procedure for first hour:

1. State overall purpose of course (see page 1 of this guide).
2. Invite participants to introduce themselves by giving their names and a *brief* statement of their expectations for this course (which the leader should make note of).
3. Building a group contract. All expectations will not be met, but hopefully everyone will have at least one of their expectations met. The key rests in willingness to read the book, be present at each session, and participate as fully as possible. Note: it is important that steps 1, 2, and 3 *not* take over 15 minutes.
4. Statement of today's purpose: In addition to the task of getting the course underway, our aim is to begin the exploration of our experience of God in the context of "process thought."
5. Divide into groups of 8 (to save time groups could be previously divided on the basis of registration) and distribute summary sheet, pencils, and paper. This group will function as the primary learning group for the remainder of the course.
6. Small group task: Begin with several minutes of silence as we bring to mind our experience of

God. Each person is then asked to write on a piece of paper three words or pictures that are evoked for them by the word "God."

7. Share these words rapidly (without challenge), recording on newsprint. Briefly note similarities and differences, affirmation and questions. Steps 4–7 need to move along rapidly in order to be completed in the 45 minutes allotted.

Procedure for second hour:

1. Continue work in small groups. Read over Pittenger's statement on "A Process View of God" (Appendix A).
2. On the basis of this statement and our own personal statements regarding our understanding of God, pose the following questions for discussion:

    a) Are we clear about what Pittenger is saying?
    b) How then does his statement affirm, challenge, or expand upon what we have said about God?
    c) What questions are left unanswered?

3. Summary statement: What two or three phrases best describe the essence of our discussion during the past hour. Note these on newsprint.

APPENDIX A:
''A PROCESS VIEW OF GOD''

"Christianity is basically a life which is lived in relationship to the way in which things *really go* in the world—and that means in relationship to what God is really 'up to' and is accomplishing in that world." (p. 22)

A. God is the chief exemplification of the following principles:

1. The world we live in is characterized by change. (p. 5)
2. If there is change, there is also temporality—to change takes time. (p. 5)
3. The world, and we ourselves in that world, is made up not of inert, changeless things, but of events and happenings. (p. 6)
4. Everything and everybody affects and influences everything and everybody else. (p. 7)
5. Freedom, in the sense of significant decisions which have consequences, runs straight through the creation. (p. 8)
6. Each occasion of energy has a di-polar quality (the abstract possibilities among which decisions must be made on the one hand, and the concrete decision and its consequences on the other). (p. 9)
7. Some events are more "important" than others. (p. 10)
8. Persuasion is stronger than sheer force or coercion. (p. 11)

B. If God is indeed "in Christ," as St. Paul puts it, then God is an active and living God who does not exist in isolation from the world and from human history. (p. 13)

C. If God is in Christ disclosed, He is disclosed as one whose nature and name is Love. (p. 17)

SESSION II: The Meaning of Humanity

Purpose: To explore in experiential terms the meaning of sin and redemption.

Procedure for first hour:

1. In total group review the summary statements prepared by each group at the conclusion of the last session. State purpose of today's session.
2. Divide into same small groups as last week. Either list on board or mimeograph for each person's use Pittenger's statement on "What it Means to be Human" (Appendix B).
3. Questions for discussion:

   a) What would you add to Pittenger's list to make it more reflective of your own experience?
   b) If this is what we are intended to be, what is it that presents us from fully "becoming what we are"?
   c) By way of summary, which of the factors we have listed produce in us the greatest feeling of helplessness and diminished sense of worth?

Procedure for second hour:

1. The purpose of this session is to explore what it means to move from the experience of helplessness and alienation talked about in the previous session to the experience of redemption witnessed to in the Gospel of Jesus Christ.
2. Each person is given a copy (or asked to refer to page 54 in this book) of the statement listed below (Appendix C).
3. In small groups, begin to explore our own experience of redemption. The following question is suggested: "How in my own life have I ex-

perienced something of that to which Dr. Pittenger refers?" In responding to this question, it might be helpful to note what "conformity to Jesus Christ" actually means in day to day experiences.

4. In bringing the session to a close, ask the group to enter into a moment of silence and then read aloud Romans 7:21–8:4, and let this serve as a summary.

APPENDIX B:
"WHAT IT MEANS TO BE HUMAN"

1. We are not so much a "being" as a "becoming."
2. We are dependent on the world in which we are set.
3. We are a mysterious and complex association of bodily stuff and mental awareness.
4. We belong to our fellow humans.
5. We possess rationality which makes us different from the animals—we think, we will, we feel.
6. We are able to love and accept love from others.
7. We have within us the implicit awareness of the reality of God.
8. We have genuine freedom to make significant decisions.

APPENDIX C:

"Many symbols have been used in Christian thought and devotion to state this enduring experience of Christian people. Some have spoken of the overcoming of the evil powers or demons which stand between God and us; others have talked about deliverance from imprisonment and the freedom of genuine sons who no longer are treated as slaves; still others have told of the injection of healthy immortal life which cures men and women from the disease and corruption which they experience apart from God. But all these are *symbols,* each of them useful at this or that time and in the light of this or that cultural milieu. The reality to which the symbols point is just one thing: it is a unity of life, on the way to full integration, where men and women are so related to what I have styled the cosmic thrust or drive, God himself, that they can go on bravely and fearlessly toward "the mark of their high calling." And what is that? Nothing other than increasing conformity to Jesus Christ himself, who is the very image of God, the one in whom divine Loving was operative with incredible speciality in a human loving which wins us and enables us to move forward as those who have become "sons in *the* Son." (p. 54)

SESSION III: A Spirit-filled Community

Purpose: To explore what it means in everyday life to be "open to the Spirit."

Procedure for first hour:

1. Write on newsprint the statement (pp. 65 and 63): "God the Holy Spirit is the mode of divine life in which God himself makes possible, through inspiration, informing, disclosing, and enabling, the right response to his outgoing Love. . . . He is present and at work everywhere."
2. Ask each person to write on a piece of paper a paragraph describing an incident in their life in which they experienced one of the following: (15 minutes)

    a. The Holy Spirit informs those who are drawn to Christ (however incognito).

    b. The Holy Spirit inspires, enlivens, strengthens the yearning of the believer, and the corporate existence of the Church as well.

    c. The Holy Spirit discloses new facets of God's character and action.

    d. The Holy Spirit enables discipleship to deepen.

3. Each person picks a partner with whom to share their description. The partner serves as a consultant to see if together they can identify what it is that was most significant in that experience. Each partner has 15 minutes to share with the other (30 minutes).

4. By way of summary, ask individuals to *call out words* that seem best to describe their experience. This is done very rapidly involving as many people as possible.

Procedure for second hour:

1. The purpose of this session is to examine some of the ways in which life in the local church enhances and might enhance more effectively that openness to the Spirit referred to in the previous session.

2. On a piece of paper each person is asked to finish the following sentence (written on the board): "My experience in church is life-giving when. . . ." (5 minutes)

3. Divide into previous small groups to share statements as they are read, have someone note them on newsprint. (15 minutes)

4. Describe briefly which of these seem to be most characteristic of our common life? Which are most unusual or difficult to come by? (20 minutes)

5. Now, on a separate piece of paper, brainstorm (see Appendix D) what might be done to increase the possibilities of genuine life-giving moments for persons in our congregation. (10 minutes)

6. Pick one item on the list that you would most like to act on. What might we do to implement this concern? (10 minutes)

APPENDIX D:
A NOTE ON BRAINSTORMING:

Brainstorming is a technique for getting as many ideas on the floor as rapidly as possible. Go around the group quickly with each person offering a comment. Everyone participates (even if to say, "I pass"). There is no discussion or critique of what is offered, nor are offerings expected to be thought out. Go around the group rapidly two or three times. The purpose is to stimulate the flow of creative energy. When the process is complete, some offerings will stand out as particularly imaginative and worth developing further.

SESSION IV: The New Life in Christ

Purpose: To explore both corporately and in ourselves what is involved in the "risk of faith."

Procedure for first hour:

1. State purpose of this final session.
2. Divide into regular working groups to respond to

the following statement by Teilhard de Chardin (quoted by Dr. Pittenger on page 81): "The problem of personal survival *per se* doesn't worry me much. Once the fruit of my life is received up into One who is eternal, what can it matter whether I am egotistically conscious of it or have joy of it? I am quite sincere when I say that my personal felicity does not interest me. To be happy it is enough to know that the best of me passes on forever into One who is more beautiful and greater than I." (Note: It might be helpful either to have their statement mimeographed or else written on newsprint for each group's use.)

3. As a statement of faith, how does this strike you? What would you have to add or change for this to express your own faith statement? (15 minutes)
4. Now, using this faith statement (however inarticulate it might seem) as a basis for your own reflection, pursue as a group the following question in whatever sequence seems comfortable.

    a. What are the risks involved in the life of faith? The obstacles (both external and internal)?
    b. What do we need from each other? What can we do to offer one another genuine support?

Procedure for second hour:

1. Continue in same groups.
2. Ask each person on a piece of paper to respond to the following statement: "At the heart of my affirmation as a Christian lies the conviction that. . . ." (15 minutes) (Note: If there is a space of time between the two hour sessions, these statements

may be prepared outside and brought to the session in the interest of time.)

3. Pair up with one other person in your group to share statements. Let your partner serve as your consultant to help you reflect on

 a. How this statement has been shaped by your experience in this course.
 b. What seems to be the "growing edge" of your faith?

Allow 30 minutes for this, 15 minutes for each person; 5 minutes to present and 10 minutes to reflect. Although this is much too short a time, the purpose is to raise issues for further reflection. It is important therefore to work strictly within the time allotted.

4. Gather into total group, form a circle, preferably standing. Begin with a moment of silence. Then ask each person to share one word or one phrase that best expresses what the experience of the course has meant for them. When everyone has spoken, conclude with an appropriate prayer of affirmation.

A WORD ABOUT EVALUATION

This course has been designed to fit (however tightly) into the time limits experienced in many congregations. If more time is available, it will, of course, loosen the process up considerably. Rather than taking session time for evaluation, it is suggested that during the week following the last session, members of the leadership team call each participant on the phone for a brief evaluation. You might want to find out:

   a. What did you find most helpful in the course?

   b. What would you omit or change if this were to be done again?

   c. What would you like to see happen in the life of our church to build on this experience?

When this information is collected, it can be passed on to those responsible for planning other programs. Of particular importance is to take seriously the suggestions offered in response to the third question. This information will be of tremendous help in overall planning. It might also be helpful to take a moment to give "feedback" to one another. How well did we work together? What did we perceive to be our individual strengths, areas of potential growth? And finally, how have we ourselves grown?

"To take the risk, and to live in terms of it, is not a guarantee of security and ease of life; but it is to build one's existence on 'something beyond the perishing of occasions.'" Amen, Come Lord Jesus!